ABOUT THE AUTHOR

Ola "Tux" Abitogun is the Creator of…

myEmpirePRO.com – A Media, Publishing, Consulting and Training Company with Internet Marketing, Networking, Electronic Medical Records and Real Estate related services. He became a FULL TIME entrepreneur in October 2006.

He is a computer engineer and an engineering management graduate from New Jersey Institute of Technology; (NJIT) class of 2004/5. He was born in Dallas Texas and raised in Nigeria by his Nigerian parents. He considers himself a proud Nigerian American.

Today, he Is a marketing addict, trainer, marketing and business consultant, real estate investor and all around serial entrepreneur.

Real Estate Money Secrets

Insider secrets to real estate investing and building a real estate empire from scratch like a PRO.

OLA TUX ABITOGUN

TERMS OF USE

Please be aware: We actively and aggressively pursue legal action against any and all persons who illegally possess or distribute this book. By purchasing or possessing this book, you agree to the Terms and Conditions listed below.

By accepting this file, book, or ebook (the "Product"), which remains the property of myEmpirePRO.com, viewing such Product, or otherwise using such Product, you (" Customer" or "you") agree to be bound by these Terms and Conditions, any terms and conditions you otherwise have entered into due to your receipt or purchase of the Product, and the terms and conditions that myEmpirePRO.com places on purchasers or users of this Product as a condition of such purchase or use.

Any earnings, income statements or other results, are based on our own testing and are only estimates of what we think you could earn. There is no assurance you will do as well as stated in any examples. If you rely upon any figures provided, you must accept the entire risk of not doing as well as the information provided.

Unless otherwise noted, you agree all content in this Product, such as text, graphics, logos, button icons, images, audio clips, digital downloads, data compilations, and software, is the property of myEmpirePRO.com or its content suppliers and protected by United States and international copyright laws. You further agree that the compilation of all content is the exclusive property of LOLAANDOLA.com. All other trademarks not owned by myEmpirePRO.com or affiliates that appear in this Product are the property of their respective owners, who may or may not be affiliated with, connected to, or sponsored by myEmpirePRO.com or its affiliates.

Only customers that have purchased this publication are authorized to view it. This publication contains material protected under International and Federal Copyright Laws and Treaties. No part of this publication may be transmitted or reproduced in any way without the prior written permission of the author. Violations of this copyright will be enforced to the full extent of the law.

You can get your own copy at
www.RealEstateMoneySecrets.com

Customer acknowledges that this Product is the confidential and proprietary information of myEmpirePRO.com and the property of myEmpirePRO.com. Customer hereby agrees to protect such confidential information. As a further condition to the purchase and/ or receipt of this Product, Customer agrees it will not, nor allow others, to directly or indirectly copy, distribute, resell, lend, lease, display, teach to others or show this Product to others.

ACKNOWLEDGEMENTS

To my beautiful wife and my kids, I love you. Thanks to my parents and extended family for doing an awesome job raising me. It's true. It takes a village. Thanks to all the numerous coaches and mentors over the years. Thanks to all the friends and family that have supported our family in prayer over the years. God bless you and your family. To God be all the glory.

Table of Content

Acknowledgements

Table of Content

Introduction

SECTION 1 - FOUNDATION & FUNDAMENTALS

    Chapter 1 - Exit Before Entry......................... 18

    Chapter 2 - Time or Money 32

    Chapter 3 - OPM & OPR.............................. 43

    Chapter 4 - Passive or Massive Income.......... 55

SECTION 2 - EXIT STRATEGIES

    Chapter 5 - Buy & Own................................ 68

    Chapter 6 - Buy & Rent................................ 78

    Chapter 7 - Wholesaling & Short Sales............ 90

Chapter 8 - Buy, Fix & Flip............................ 101

Chapter 9 - Buy, Fix & Rent........................... 115

Chapter 10 - Subject To & Rent to Own........... 126

Chapter 11 - Mortgage Notes........................ 136

SECTION 3 - ENTRY STRATEGIES (Finding Deals)

Chapter 12 - On & Off Market Deals............... 148

Chapter 13 - Auctions & Foreclosure Sales...... 159

Chapter 14 - Agency & M.L.S........................ 166

Chapter 15 - Online Ads & PPC..................... 172

Chapter 16 - 7 Keys to Success..................... 180

Conclusion

References

Notes

INTRODUCTION

It was 2004. I was graduating with a computer engineering degree from NJIT. However, the future wasn't as clear as it once was when I started college.

I was being offered the 40-40-40-40 plan: $40,000 annual salary, working 40 hours a week to pay off a $40,000 student loan. Judging by the looks of things, I might have to work for 40 years before I can even remotely think of retirement.

I believe we can both agree now that a career as a real estate investor was and still is a better choice. If you didn't feel that way, chances are you would not be reading this book. But let me share my personal 'why' with you.

You can call me ungrateful, but the 40-40-40-40 plan felt like sophisticated slavery to me. I lost all passion for the idea of becoming a $100,000 per year engineer. The math simply wasn't adding up.

I began researching the idea of becoming my own boss, and it just made sense to pursue a career that doesn't cap my potential income.

By selling my personal time rather than delivering results, I would inevitably end up in a never-ending cycle. I only have so many hours in a day.

I did the math with a very optimistic ideal: $100 per hour. What if I were getting paid $100 per hour for my time and skills as a professional? What if I were a superman who could work 24 hours a day without needing sleep? That would mean I couldn't make more than $2,400 in any given day.

If I worked every day of the year, I would never be able to make more than $878,400 in any year. Again, I am assuming every year is a leap year. I would never make up to $1 million in a year in a career that depends on selling time. I knew I could do better, and I certainly wanted to do better.

Over the years, things have become more consolidated and have taken on greater meaning for me. Today, I know that the money I make is directly proportional to the value I add to others or the number of people I serve.

I know I can provide much more value beyond $1 million per year. So clearly, if all I know how to do is sell my time like most 9-5 professions, it's an indication that I am not worth $1 million per year.

The question that kept me intrigued was, "How could I increase my value in the marketplace?" The only answer to that question was selling results.

Sure, results take time to achieve. But if I continue to innovate and create new ways to produce results faster, it means more income for me within the same period of time.

However, if all I am selling is time, employers will only give me more work whenever I figure out new ways to get things done faster. My income would essentially remain the same since I get paid by the hour.

These thoughts got me intrigued about entrepreneurship in general. As for real estate specifically, I stumbled into it. But stumbling into it wasn't enough to stay in it when the whole market crashed in 2008.

Money can be a motivation to get into real estate investing. But I am warning you right now, it won't be enough to help you stay in it.

I fell in love with the idea and the prospect of making $30,000 per deal. However, it was crickets between December 2004 and December 2005. Finally, I closed my first deal in December 2005.

As soon as I started taking action, I quickly realized that I had learned lots of gimmicks from the gurus that just wouldn't work 99% of the time in the real world. My goal in this book is to help you skip all these time-wasting gimmicks.

As I mentioned, I stumbled into real estate. I made lots of money (upwards of $3 million in transactions), but it all got wiped out by 2009. After that, I decided to choose real estate from an educated standpoint. I will be sharing more of the stories throughout this book.

Most people look at real estate from a sentimental and emotional standpoint. My goal is to help you start looking at it from an objective but profit-oriented standpoint.

Your number one asset as a human being is your time. But at the top of that list is real estate. What's common with personal time and real estate? You cannot create more of either.

We all have 24 hours per day as individuals and can't possibly create more. Available land on Earth is also limited while the population is growing. Every other type of asset can be duplicated, reproduced, and therefore devalued.

Historically, real estate continues to grow in value, and that's not going to stop anytime soon. In my opinion, it's the best industry to learn and use to grow your net worth.

Many people have lost money big time in real estate. As I mentioned earlier, I was in the middle of the 2008 recession, and I lost everything. Lol... I wasn't ready.

The primary reason why people lose in real estate is not knowing the proper way to enter and/or exit. Using real estate as the cookie-cutter American dream vehicle is obsolete. Today, there is more to it.

In this book, I will focus on sharing stories that educated me on how to identify entry and exit points in real estate transactions, either for personal use or investment purposes. Real estate affects your net worth and bottom-line income, whether you know it or not.

In section 1, I will cover some foundational and fundamental concepts to ensure that we are on the same page. There are some core concepts that we have to agree on before moving forward. Not agreeing on these concepts will have a downstream effect on the overall takeaway.

Then section 2 will cover exit strategies starting from a home you purchase for personal use. We will end this section with an understanding of mortgage notes as a money-making tool for the banks. After this chapter, you too can now make money from them.

Last but not least, 80% of the knowledge in this book will be useless to you if you don't master the information in section 3. There are special opportunities in real estate that can only be found through unconventional methods. No other book is sharing them quite like this.

I have been known to be quite awesome at breaking down complex concepts into simple understandable language. This book will not be any different. Real estate wealth strategies can be quite intimidating. In fact, there are many seminars around the world that charge upwards of $40,000 for a weekend to learn the content of this book. No worries, you now have the key in your hands.

I am very aware that most people will never take action on the content. That's very much okay because that's exactly why there is always room for those who choose to execute. The numbers, risks, rewards, and competition level work out just fine for everyone.

Starting with chapter 1, we will break down the number 1 rule: exit before entry. It's the first chapter for a reason. It's extremely easy to break this rule. It's also the best and easiest way to lose money in real estate endeavors of any type.

See you in the first section starting with chapter 1.

SECTION 1

FOUNDATION & FUNDAMENTALS

CHAPTER 1

Exit Before Entry

Luckily enough for me, this was one of the first lessons that I learned from one of my real estate early days mentors, Richard Douglas. This is one of those rules that you will often see the teacher breaking in spite of the fact that the consequences can be deadly.

Here is why. It's just that easy of a rule to break. But as I said, it's a deadly mistake that most people make when engaging in any type of real estate investing.

I can't stress it enough; you must predetermine your exit strategy before entering into a deal. That's what *"exit before entry"* means.

Is that common sense? Unfortunately it is not. If you are a normal human being like the rest of us, you have to continuously remind yourself of this rule. It's easy to forget and break the rule.

"There are two times in a man's life when he should not speculate; when he can't afford it and when he can." ~ Mark Twain

It's in our nature to speculate. That's why speculation sells. Think about the hottest selling products since the history of mankind. It's usually hope or speculation driven.

These products and services can usually not be proven objectively or factually to actually deliver value. They are usually unproven promises made by other humans to you. You can see examples of these in religion and politics.

I will stay clear of religion as an example here because I have my own faith that I would want others to respect.

But mind you, that's why it is called faith. It is the evidence of things not seen.

When it comes to entrepreneurship, you will need faith a lot. Your path to results is not always going to be so straightforward. Obstacles that look like a complete end to the journey will often appear in your path.

But there is a thin line between your need for faith and straight up speculation in your real estate investment. When you cross this line by entering real estate deals without determining your exit strategy, disasters will occur.

The masses experienced such a catastrophe in 2008. It was completely avoidable. But they sold speculations to everyone starting a few years prior to that.

It is in fact true that real estate has consistently grown in value historically speaking. But you have to keep in mind that history is across multiple lifetimes.

If your entry and exit period falls within the wrong window of time in history, you can lose financial stability for decades.

Real estate agents and mortgage officers were selling everyone on the speculation that every real estate investment will appreciate. This is called *"half lie half*

truth." Over time, all real estate will appreciate. Your particular investment may not.

> *"Speculation is only a word covering the making of money out of the manipulation of prices, instead of supplying goods and services."* ~ Henry Ford

There is a difference between price and value. Value transcends multidimensionally. As long as we value shelter, we as human race will continue to be willing to pay a little more for housing; especially with inflation in the equation.

Price however is time sensitive based on what the general market feels a piece of real estate is worth at any particular moment. It's a grand measure of the fear and confidence in the marketplace at any particular time. Timing is essentially everything.

It is important for you to know that price *(camouflaged as value)* can be manipulated by influential entities.

Federal reserve and central banks are major factors because of their control on interest rates and inflation. These are factors that affect the value of your cash currency.

The real estate market can be overbought or oversold relative to actual intrinsic value. It can be overpriced or underpriced. Therefore there is a particular formula to determine what side of the trade you want to fall in; win or lose.

In any trade or investment, someone is always the sucker. It's usually the speculator. It's usually the person who doesn't believe there is a sucker involved in the trade.

I am not saying that you should be out to hurt others. All I am suggesting is for you to avoid being the sucker by determining the exit strategy before entering the deal. It's the first step in your due diligence.

Here is a harsh reality. In order to have a sustainable market place, values have to consolidate across multidimensional preferences. Market crashes happen when a significant section of the market focuses on too similar dimensions.

An example is when it becomes an over-popular idea to invest in real estate at a particular moment. Most people are not analyzing their exit strategies properly. They just want to be a part of a popular idea.

When you enter a commercial building, you can clearly see the exit signs. However residential code doesn't require much enforcement of that. The reason is because exit related risks and liabilities are significantly higher in big commercial buildings.

This comparison is a great analogy for comparison between your savings bank account and real estate investment. It's easier to exit one than the other. You can walk into your bank and withdraw all your cash anytime you want and walk out with it.

When you enter into a real estate deal, the process of exiting is not so simple. You have to find a willing and able buyer to sell the property to. That process can take 60-90 days on the market provided that it is priced right.

Expect that process to take longer if the listing is not priced right. Every now and then, sellers would wait around for that 90 days of the property on that market to feel the reality of the true value of their property. Within that holding time, the cost of ownership of the property continues to incur.

For example, the ownership of a single family in Roselle New Jersey may cost you around $12,000 in annual property taxes payable to the city of Roselle. Imagine entering into a deal and then trying to exit. You've decided to list the property at $250,000.

90 days after your real estate agent listed the property, you have not received a single offer close enough to your asking price. At that point, you've now heard the market clearly indicating that you are delusional for thinking that your property is worth $250,000. But the lesson is not over.

That delusion has cost you a whole 90 days of taxes that you now have incurred in additional cost; one quarter of $12,000. That's $3,000. There are 20 or more other types of costly mistakes like this that you can make when you don't obey the rules of **"exit before entry."**

Speculators never see this coming. They have usually emotionally bought into the idea of becoming a successful real estate investor. That's an attachment to the sentiments.

In reality, successful real estate investors create and follow rules. They do so because they are 100% aware of their emotional nature with the need for a guide against self destruction by speculation. Without this guide, the downstream effect of speculation on your real estate portfolio can be devastating.

So one primary job you have now is identifying the spirit of speculation. If you find yourself saying things like *"it just makes too much sense to not be a deal"* when I ask you what the potential R.O.i is. chances are you are a speculator. That's an awesome way to lose lots of money.

Instead, you need to identify and know your numbers. Beyond your numbers, you should always add a 5-10% error buffer for "just in case". In real estate, costly surprises are inevitable.

There is a fine line between conservatism and the required due diligence in successful real estate investing. Sometimes, you just have to wait for the right deal. While waiting for the right deal, it may be tempting to jump in the wrong deal. You may even be made fun of as scared.

You may hear things like *"scared money don't make money."* That's not applicable to you if you have an active pipeline where you are actively scouting for good deals.

What is a good deal?

A good deal is a deal with a clear and explicit exit strategy before you enter it. It's very hard to see the true map of navigating a forest when you are already inside it. Know your exit before entering the deal.

If you want to take it a step or notch up, have backup exit strategies for your deals as well. This is how to protect the empire and your money. Sales agents will try to make you feel guilty for doing your due diligence. Don't fall for it.

Fill up your pipeline with potential prospects and obey the Warren Buffet rule; *"never lose money."* Here is how. Create an airtight prequalification process that doesn't depend on value appreciation.

Value appreciation and equity growth should be the added bonus for you. Dependency on this type of value gain in your investments is 100% speculation. Besides, you can't determine a profitable exit strategy with value appreciation unless you know how to see the future.

If you can see the future, you don't need real estate. You would be better off in the stock market. The beauty in real estate investing is the ability to buy low and sell high.

Selling high becomes the default when you master the art and science of buying lower than market value as you will learn in the rest of this book. You will also learn how to add value to properties a.k.a create value out of thin air. With this strategy, you win 100% of the time. This lesson is simply to ensure your exit before you enter.

Sometimes, you may encounter potential leads with little to *'not enough data'* to make a buying decision. That usually means not having enough when it's time to exit the deal as well. It makes it that much difficult to determine your exit strategy right?

Avoid such deals. If you can't find enough data, it's an indication that there is not enough market. Some interpret that as low competition. Contrary to popular belief, low competition is an indication and/or sign that you will lose money if you engage in such business.

In the next chapter, you will learn the two different types of resources you have available to play in real estate. I will show you how to best allocate them for best returns in the shortest possible amount of time.

Everyone can and should be building their financial profile in part or whole using real estate. There are no entry barriers. Therefore it is easy to take for granted. With or without credit or money, it's an even playground for every and anyone.

3 PRO T1PS: How To Get The Most Value Out of this Book.

You got through the first chapter. Congratulations.

Are you like me, easily distracted when you're reading? Well, I've got some awesome tricks up my sleeve to help you make the most of this book. Let's dive into them.

Okay, here's the first trick: never stop in the middle of a chapter. Why, you ask? Because finishing a chapter feels like a little victory! It's like reaching a checkpoint in a video game. And who doesn't love achievements, right?

When you complete a chapter, it's like a high-five from your brain, saying, "Great job, keep going!" So, even if you stumble upon a tricky part, power through and finish that chapter. You'll be all set to start fresh with the next one, and you'll feel amazing doing it!

Now, let me drop another cool life hack on you. Imagine this: you're not just reading a book; you're also listening to it at the same time. How cool is that? Well, it's not just cool; it's super effective!

When you listen to an audiobook while reading the physical book or ebook, your brain goes into overdrive. It's like you're downloading information into multiple parts of your brain at once. Fancy, right? This is how I tackle books that are totally worth reading.

Plus, if you're someone like me who sometimes struggles to stay focused, this hack is a game-changer. The audio keeps you engaged, preventing those pesky zoning-out moments. I even recorded this book out loud over two days, just so you don't have to struggle like I did.

So, if you want to give it a shot, grab the audio version and try it out. You'll be amazed at how valuable this technique can be!

I wanted to share this "hack" with you right at the start. Why? Because I believe in giving you the best tools right away. If you found this first chapter valuable enough to keep your attention, you're in for a fantastic journey.

Oh, and one more thing to keep in mind: we don't update the audio books as quickly as the text versions, so hop on this opportunity early!

There you have it, friends. With these tricks, you'll be on your way to getting the most out of this book. Happy reading and learning!

PS & A BONUS: *Read the book more than once and you will learn something new every single time.*

CHAPTER 2

Time or Money

I hear it all the time. *"I don't have the time. I don't have the skills. I don't have the money. I don't have the desire..."* and so on. If there's one thing we excel at as people, it's pointing out our thousands of legitimate excuses.

Personally, I think all excuses are legitimate. However, that doesn't mean it serves you to use your very legitimate excuses as an excuse not to build your real estate portfolio. With that being said, the only excuse you should allow yourself to use is a lack of desire.

I doubt you would be reading this book if you didn't have some level of desire to invest in real estate for profits. At the very least, you would want to buy your personal residence in real estate at the best deal possible. That means you possess all the prerequisites you need to be able to do this.

When I first encountered real estate back in 2004, I knew it was going to be a fun journey; the first of its kind for me. As I said earlier, I was finishing my senior year at NJIT (New Jersey Institute of Technology) at the time. Outside of organizing musical concerts as a young musician, I knew it was another opportunity to express my artistic and creative energy.

Sure enough, within the next year, I created tools and methodologies to help me execute marketing and facilitate deals faster and easier than the status quo. I still do that to this day. In fact, the publishing of my wealth of knowledge in this book is one of those moves. Surprise! There is an agenda.

My parents were not wealthy by human standards. I was raised in a modest household. We weren't poor either. My father and mother were professional teachers.

I guess some things are starting to make sense now. But they had dreams of me becoming a doctor or architect. Clearly, I wasn't equipped with knowledge, tools, and ready-made resources to become a successful real estate investor.

The resource I had was time; 24 hours per day. I started like everyone else. We were having a simple conversation, and my pastor's wife mentioned real estate.

Instantly, I manufactured an excuse. *"I have bad credit,"* I said. When you create your next excuse, I want you to note one thing. It's a sign that you have not mastered how to stay in the present.

My pastor's wife simply suggested an opportunity. Instead of asking how I could benefit from it starting now, my mind traveled into my past to dig up why I shouldn't do it.

Thank God she had a saving grace response. Once I said I had bad credit, she told me it doesn't matter. Then I knew I was on to something.

I took to the internet to do a little research. As you can imagine, I stumbled into tons of information on how I could make a fortune in real estate. It all made sense to me.

I could buy houses and rent them out for the rest of my life. Not quite exactly but close enough to my idea of making money from creating results; a roof over the head.

Then I asked another friend of mine. He referred me to another event he had heard about. It was from an organization called NIDA in East Orange, New Jersey, organized for first-time homebuyers.

I attended and decided to hang out and ask more questions after the event. One of the sponsors, who was a mortgage officer, claimed I could buy a house with a credit score as low as 500.

I booked an appointment to see a house in Belleville, New Jersey, with a realtor. Once she showed up, I realized we had met before at some other entrepreneur wannabe seminar.

Anyway, the Belleville house was a single-family home that needed some TLC (Tender Loving Care). It needed simple stuff like new carpeting and painting. I thought, *"Wow, this is so easy."*

From what I learned at the NIDA event, I could buy this at any price and rent it out. Clearly, there was more to what makes that a profitable venture deal. It didn't matter; I was excited.

I called one of my best friends while the realtor was showing me the house. He had been helping his mom manage a couple of multifamily houses in Newark and Orange, New Jersey. I thought he would know much more from his experience.

A partnership with an experienced person seemed ideal to me. But he didn't seem as excited as I was. I am glad I did not buy that house because it would have been a total disaster. How? You will find out by the end of reading this book.

Have you ever bought a new car and started noticing that everyone else has that same car afterward? It happens every time you buy into a new idea. You will start noticing related stuff everywhere after that.

After these encounters, I started noticing everything real estate-related. A few weeks later, I stumbled into an infomercial on late-night TV. The call to action was to redeem a free ticket to a free seminar on how to make money in real estate.

I went as far as I could through the sales funnel and ended up with a $3,000 course. I received a bunch of binders and an email address for email coaching. I don't remember ever getting a reply to my emails.

But I got one solid tip. That tip was to join a local real estate association club, which I did. From there, I met two mentors who helped make the three years after that highly profitable; over $3 million in transactions.

What's the moral of this story? In order to make any type of money, some kind of value was invested. Some cash was involved, but it was mainly time that I invested.

I had a strong desire to begin with, but it was simply a desire and will to invest the required time. Alternatively, you may not have time because you are stuck in a 9-5 job. It's extremely difficult to spend 10-12 hours on your day job and then come back home and not be able to relax.

In that case, I would hope that the said job is paying you at least $40,000 in annual salary. Either way, you have to be willing to invest some money into learning, marketing, and possibly partnership. The idea is to leverage money.

If you have the prerequisite, strong enough desire, then you are willing and able to invest either time, money, or a hybrid of both in real estate. It's that simple to make some serious money. At the minimum, you can buy your personal home at an incredible discount or with built-in equity.

Credit? That falls under money. Credit is just another source of money. If you are like me, I didn't have a good credit rating when I got started. Once I started making some money, my credit rating reflected that.

If you already have a good credit rating, that's great. It simply means you have access to more money to invest in the real estate game.

When it comes to using money to increase your financial profile in real estate, the amount of money you have in your savings or bank account is not relevant. What's more relevant is the amount of money that you have access to. Once you understand how profound that is, that understanding is a game-changer.

The whole real estate game is about learning how to flip time and money into more income. The best part about all that is that it doesn't have to be your personal time or your personal money.

As you continue into this book, I will share multiple different ways that you can gain much more access to other people's time and money. We cover that in detail in chapter 3.

You've taken a great step in investing one or two of these resources in getting this book. Contrary to popular belief, the greatest thing you can invest in is not the house you live in. It's in yourself.

In fact, I was just watching a young lady on YouTube who invested $90,000 in a seminar on the topic I am sharing in this book. As usual, she dropped out of the program without trying to get her money back. But there is an even more important lesson to learn here.

In no way, shape, or form am I asking you to go find a guru to spend $90,000 with. More importantly, think about a person who thinks there is so much value that they are willing to invest that amount of money. These types of individuals probably think they will get a minimum of $90,000 in some type of value back; probably monetarily.

So I don't know how much you've invested in this book. I'm sure it's probably less than $30. What would that return on investment be if you could make $90,000 after a year? That would be almost 300,000%.

Investing in learning the real estate money game is one of the only few areas where that's possible. So remember, it's not about how much time, money, and resources that you personally possess. It's completely irrelevant.

It's about how resourceful you can get. How much money and time can you create access to? You will learn the various ways to do that in this book. Be mindful that most people will never get this. Congratulations.

You may not have invested $90,000 in learning this stuff. But if I were you, I'd pretend that I have invested $200,000 into my real estate education. What that does is drive your anger and hunger levels to create a massive and unusual result.

It's a scientific fact that people only value things that are difficult to get. If you got this book as a free download, there is a heightened chance that you won't create results from the information in it. You can create results, however, if you pretend that you paid $90,000 for it.

Your personal time is very precious because it's limited to only 24 hours in a day. However, it's a form of energy. Energy is neither created nor destroyed. So even though it may seem that you are losing time, usually, it's been expended in areas of your life that may not be so profitable. I guarantee you that someone is making millions of dollars from your personal time if you are not.

When you decide to invest your time and money in yourself through this type of personal development education, it can pay off massively. That's simply energy changing forms. It's similar to water changing forms from water to gas and to ice.

It's important for me to explain this to you because how you choose to invest this resource henceforth will determine if it's truly limited or unlimited.

I used to say we have limited resources. But as I grew in the journey, I realized it was a limiting belief system. You and I do in fact have unlimited resources to invest in real estate. I'll prove that to you in the next chapter.

CHAPTER 3

OPM & OPR

What is OPM and OPR? Low-key, I am hoping that you are already familiar with the concept of other people's money. But I will not assume. Let's get into it.

OPM stands for Other People's Money. Have you ever heard the saying that it takes money to make money? Often, people say that as an excuse to not get started in launching a business.

There is only one scenario I can think of where this statement would be true. That's when no one else believes in your money-making idea. Most business ideas are fruitless, so I can understand why people would say that.

Clearly, real estate investment is not a fruitless business idea. If, for some weird reason, you feel it is fruitless, that will get cleared up by the time you finish reading this book.

But beyond that, you may be limited to only funds you own if you don't have trust equity with other sources of funds. An example of trust equity is your credit score or ratings. It's a way for the owner of funds to determine your level of trustworthiness.

So it goes back to the same thing. Your source of money (OPM) has to believe in you and your idea. "Believe" is actually the wrong word. It's more like your trust equity, worthiness, ratings, or score.

Real estate is a real business. In any circumstance, you will find yourself as a buyer, seller, service provider, or facilitator. In any of these roles, trust or your belief must be irrelevant unless measurable equity of some type is involved.

So it's your responsibility to build your trust equity in a measurable and trackable way for the real estate marketplace. That's the number one way to get unlimited access to other people's money.

So we are trying to learn real estate money secrets. How does this knowledge translate to net income for you?

Let's go through some numbers to give you a clear understanding of the application of OPM in real estate investing.

If you figured out a proven way to turn $100 into $130 in real estate investing, that's an opportunity that other individuals and even big institutions would love to capitalize on. What if you can turn around and sell each of these opportunities at $5 each?

I will give you my $100, you will turn it into $130. Of course, I am happy to pay you $5 each time this same scenario plays out successfully like this.

My net profit is then $30 minus a fee of $5, which is equal to $25. That's also a return on investment (ROI) of $25 (the profit) divided by $100 (the initial investment) and then multiplying the result by 100%; that's 25%.

(25/100) x 100 = 25% R.O.I.

So let's assume that you only have $200 in your personal possession. That limits your potential income to $60 for each revenue cycle, right? That would be...

30% of $200 initial investment = $60 profit

That's not bad, but it can be better if you have access to "other people's money" (OPM). After all, it's a proven profitable real estate investment vehicle. So let's assume that you are able to source $100 each from 7 of your friends.

Remember that each one of them will basically expect a 25% ROI because you've got to feed your family too. You've decided to charge them 5% for your investment management fees. Let's figure out how much additional profit that would be for you.

7 Friends x $100 initial investment each = $700 in Total Initial Investment

Net Profit (25% of $700) = $175

Sure, you have helped all these people to make $175 in total; pure profit. But more importantly, you just made additional money from leveraging other people's money. How much exactly?

    Net Profit to You (5% of $700) = $35.

The return on investment for this money for you is nearly infinite (∞) because the initial investment was not your personal money. You only invested in creating your proven system and expertise. You could have decided to charge more and even charge up to 50% of the profit.

In fact, let's do the math if you had charged 15% and netted the investor 15%. It's a very fair game. You are helping them put their money to work. Here is the difference in the return on investment with that change.

    7 Friends x $100 initial investment each = $700 in Total Initial Investment

    Net Profit to Investors (15% of $700) = $105

    Net Profit to You (15% of $700) = $105.

Remember that you had invested your own personal $200 to make a net of $60. That ROI was 30% as usual.

(60/200) x 100 = 30% R.O.I.

It's your money, but you also facilitated the investment. (25% + 5% = 30%).

But for investing in your education on how money works with real estate and putting that to work for others, you have significantly increased your effective ROI.

Let's do that calculation. Your initial investment is still $200. However, your effective profit has increased by $105, making it a total profit of $165 ($60 + $105).

(165/200) x 100 = 82.5% R.O.I.

Your effective return on investment for having and/or creating access to OPM (other people's money) went from 30% ROI to 82.5% ROI. That is a 175% increase in net income.

((82.5% - 30%)/30%) x 100 = 175% Increase.

The effect of applying O.P.M to your real estate investment is exponential. Some people call it the compound effect. Discover what happens when you increase $100 by 175% 10 times.

	$100.00		$275.00
	$275.00		$825.00
	$825.00		$2,475.00
	$2,475.00		$7,425.00
	$7,425.00		$22,275.00
	$22,275.00		$66,825.00
	$66,825.00		$200,475.00
	$200,475.00		$601,425.00
	$601,425.00		$1,804,275.00
	$1,804,275.00		$5,412,825.00
	$5,412,825.00		$16,238,475.00

It grows to $16 million+. It's mind boggling; I know but it's simple math. You can apply this as soon as you are ready. But I'm afraid that you won't be able to apply this ancient secret in any linear endeavor such as a 9-5 job.

You should also be aware that most business ideas that involve just you and the money you own personally cannot leverage this ancient phenomenon. What happens when we double the number of investors? Let's find out.

7**x2** Friends x $100 initial investment each

= $1,400 in Total Initial Investment

Net Profit to Investors (**15%** of $1,400) = $210

Net Profit to You (15% of $1,400) = $210.

Your effective profit has increased by $210 making it a total profit of $270.

(270/200) x 100 = 135% R.O.I

Effectively, your R.O.I went from 30% R.O.I to 135% R.O.I. That is a 350% increase in net income.

((135% - 30%)/30%) x 100 = 350% Increase. Let's find out what happens to that table when $100 grows by 350% ten times.

	$100.00	$450.00
	$450.00	$2,025.00
	$2,025.00	$9,112.50
	$9,112.50	$41,006.25
	$41,006.25	$184,528.13
	$184,528.13	$830,376.56
	$830,376.56	$3,736,694.53
	$3,736,694.53	$16,815,125.39
	$16,815,125.39	$75,668,064.26
	$75,668,064.26	$340,506,289.16
	$340,506,289.16	$1,532,278,301.22

That $100 grows to $1.5 Billion. That's called exponential growth. By now, it should start making sense to you why the bank is in the business of giving you a free savings account.

We need to take this concept a bit further into the OPR (other people's resources). It gets even better. Money is not the only resource that turns an investment into profits.

Time and money turns into other forms of energy and it's your responsibility to manage the energy in its different forms. That ability is what sets the winners and losers apart from a financial standpoint.

If you dig enough online, you will find videos where I am advising my followers that they have limited resources and it's in fact a reason for resource management in one's life. I've grown a bit more since then.

In reality, we all can create access to unlimited resources as demonstrated with the numbers I illustrated in the figures above. It's about being resourceful. Every successful empire in the history of mankind has leveraged some kind of credit.

They trade with other empires, lend and borrow from each other because it is the most profitable thing to do. If you've learned to stay always within your means, you need to let go of that and start thinking a little bigger.

Just like many other myths we've bought into from childhood, the reality is that it's often opposite what it seems. If not, we won't have to figure out new concepts daily.

Without leveraging OPM and OPR, it's virtually impossible for you to create above and beyond average types of results. The alternative is to play it safe and live within your means for life. There is nothing wrong with that but you cannot maximize the exponentially multiplying power of OPM & OPR with such behavior.

It's the very reason why collaborations, partnerships and joint ventures are some of the most profitable concepts to ever be discovered by humans.

In the next chapter, we will take it a little further. We will talk about the differences between making big money and making money in your sleep no matter how small it is. One is not necessarily better than the other, but you need to be clear on the differences.

CHAPTER 4

Passive or Massive Income

One of the biggest mistakes I made in my real estate journey is particularly and directly sourced from my understanding of the correlation between passive and massive income. I heard that cash is king for the longest but it's half truth. My goal in this chapter is to shed some light on the fast that cash is dead money all by itself.

When I read [Rich Dad Poor Dad by Robert Kiyosaki](#) and [Secrets of a Millionaire Mind by T Harv Eker](#) back in 2005, I learned about residual and passive income. At the time, they sounded like the best thing since sliced bread.

However, as soon as my career took off in December 2005 with my first $10,000 check, I completely forgot about the idea of making money in my sleep. A $10,000 check was a massive income. The next check after that was about $23,000.

I started closing deals, and over the next 25 deals, I averaged about $30,000 per deal, with the highest check from one deal being $82,000. Who has time to think about passive and residual income when you could just make $30,000 checks? It was good, and it made it easy to get lost because I really was feeling invisible.

Then in 2007, deal flow started to slow down. A friend of mine and mentor, Bob Baeranbach, warned me about what was coming. But of course, I didn't listen.

Bob was and is still one of my most trusted mortgage bankers. In my mind at the time, he didn't understand what I understood about the real estate streets. Money was available from the bank, and I thought life would continue like that.

In fact, I am not ashamed to confess today that I never heard the word "recession" before Bear Stearns and Lehman Brothers, multi-billion-dollar finance operations, crashed in 2008. The party was over, but I was in denial. Let me share how easy it was with you to get money for real estate acquisitions.

Once I found a deal and an end buyer with an okay credit score, the bank only needed a good appraisal to justify the loan-to-value ratio of the deal. They didn't care about income level or income verification. Real estate value was hot because more buyers were coming into the marketplace.

As a young 27-year-old with 2 years of consistent success, I thought it would last forever. I really did. But suddenly, my mortgage officers would check credit, but deals would not get through underwriting. Deals that were taking 20 days or less were now stretching beyond 45 days before we got a declined application.

It became clear to me that I had lost my way into a world of fantasy. Don't get me wrong, those were real money made between December 2005 and October/November 2008. I personally created over $3 million in real estate transactions within my first 24 months.

From one perspective, I can say it was a setup for failure. But from the best perspective, it was a great way to learn the business. But I have to say I was lucky.

I didn't live a flamboyant lifestyle. I had colleagues and friends who did. They were riding in luxury and exotic cars. One of my closest friends, who was actually my first mentor, had monthly expenses up to $25,000.

You can only imagine how bad his financial profile was hit when all those massive paydays disappeared. It was bad. It wasn't bad for me because I had savings that lasted me many months, and bills paid for multiple households for over a year.

Eventually, money started going low in my bank accounts. So I started to snap out of the amnesia. I was confused, but I knew that being confused meant that it's time to learn something new.

As I was starting to study the greats again just like I did back in 2005, I noticed that Warren Buffet and many other wealthy people make money every time a can of Coca

Cola is sold. Even better, every time a Geico Insurance subscriber pays their monthly bill, Warren Buffett gets paid a certain amount of money.

That's residual and passive income. I knew that I had to leverage the downtime to structure passive and residual income into what I already knew how to do. So basically, my whole million-dollar real estate operation had just crashed and burned, and I blamed it all on the lack of passive and residual income.

What was the alternative? I flipped over 40 deals, and many of them could have been structured to create monthly cash flow from rental income. Knowing what I know today, some of those $30,000 paydays could have been structured into part massive and part passive income.

In addition to owning a few rental properties, I could have set up additional passive and residual income from helping others. There were many clients who didn't have the time to manage their rental properties. I could have charged a fee of 10% of the rental cash flow or more to facilitate these services.

When I think back, I am glad that my first operation crashed the way it did. I needed the reminder. A business without monthly consistent cash flow is basically destined to fail.

When the real estate market crashed in 2008, many of the people that were capitalizing on the boom before that got desperate. Many mortgage officers, real estate agents, attorneys, and closing agents started using desperate measures to do very shady deals.

I heard of many scenarios where people created fake social security numbers. They nurtured credit ratings with these fake profiles. I heard of many who took out hundreds of thousands of dollars in mortgage loans, paid the mortgage for 6 months, and then abandoned the homes to go into foreclosure.

Once I started hearing this craziness, I decided to exit the real estate business altogether. That was in 2009. I got on a mission to create a business that's structured around residual and passive income.

I started doing research on internet marketing as a means to that end. Pay per click was the first strategy I learned. I lost $700 in 5 minutes messing around with Google AdWords and made my first $23 or so. Even though I was negative net profit $667, it felt good, and I knew I was on to something big.

So why was I excited about a $23 sale when I was used to $30,000 paydays? I'll tell you why. I was trying to set up a $23 per minute residual income machine. That means $23 that comes in every minute even while I am sleeping.

You see, even if it was $23 per hour, multiply $23 by 24 hours per day. That will be $552 per day, which is $16,000+ per month in residual and passive income. The best part about this type of income is that it is generated from recession-proof sales.

- Do we still have to eat during a recession?

- Are we all still obligated to pay the insurance on our cars in a recession?
- Do we still have to pay our rent in a recession even if we lose our source of income?

If all these answers are 'yes,' I knew I had to restructure my business and my real estate empire.

While it was great to have those massive paydays, my business was at the mercy of a great economy. As I was still trying to figure out internet marketing, my real estate mentor introduced me to a home-based business opportunity called ACN. It was an opportunity to distribute phone services. Isn't phone services another thing we continue to pay for, even in a recession? It is.

So it aligned with what I was trying to do. The only problem was that the business model depended on my ability to recruit others starting with my family and friends. So in an effort to avoid the idea of dependency on family and friends, I stumbled right back into internet marketing.

It was now September 2009. With an edge of attraction science, things made a little more sense, and I thrived in really mastering internet marketing. Combining internet marketing and sales skills with my background in computer engineering became very useful.

I had $3,000 paydays and even built my revenue from selling simple information products back up to $40,000. This was generated from selling simple membership products for as low as $97 per month. It was residual and passive, but once again something was missing.

These were still products that weren't necessities. They were informational products. Great products to sell and a great business model with low overhead cost. But the business is not recession-proof.

So between 2010 and 2013, there were lots of ups and downs. The good news was that I was learning all along those mistakes. My conclusion by 2014 was that both massive and passive income are both always necessary.

Recession-proof passive income is necessary as regular cash flow because monthly bills do not care. Those things keep coming in. Sometimes, business is slow, and the first thing that halts is massive purchases. No one is trying to make big purchases when there is no confidence in the marketplace. When news starts breaking everywhere that an economic recession is coming, people stop spending money on certain things.

But with passive income, sometimes a massive income can become an awesome initial investment to build out passive income. So with my experience and expertise, it made sense to find a way to leverage internet marketing in real estate.

That's what I'm up to these days. In 2014, I realized that I've learned so much in marketing that would be applicable to securing bargains in real estate. The idea is to use my marketing skills to find and prequalify deals at $0.70 (70 cents) or less on the dollar. While I can sell for a nice $10,000 payday, I can retain some for rental cash flow, and I can also help others who do not have the time to manage their properties.

It's easy to get comfortable when you know how to flip properties for massive paydays. I know how to, and in the rest of this book, I share the strategies with you. But it's dangerous when you don't structure it around a growing monthly recession-proof cash flow.

Likewise, many people start building a rental property portfolio with a job mindset. The idea is to grow the portfolio as fast as possible. If you master how to have massive paydays, your bank account will pre-qualify you for acquiring more properties.

For every $10,000 you add to your bank account, your purchasing power increases by $30,000. As I shared with you in the chapter on OPM & OPR, it makes the bank feel a lot more comfortable in giving you money for more deals. The more rental units you own, the more cash flow your real estate portfolio produces.

Massive and passive real estate income work hand in hand. Set up your real estate journey to benefit from both of them. There will be surprises but everything will be insured against any type of market calamities.

In the next section, we will dive into exit strategies. Hopefully, by now, I've managed to sell you exiting before entering. These are the ways to plan for massive and passive profits before getting into any irreversible and/or deadly situation.

Let's keep it moving.

SECTION 2

EXIT STRATEGIES

CHAPTER 5

Buy & Own

As I mentioned earlier, Rent is one of the expenses that we all have to incur monthly regardless of what condition the economy is in. How sweet would it be if you can flip that concept from root to the head to add to your bottom line? Wouldn't that be awesome?

In this chapter, you will discover how to leverage real estate to improve your financial profile by replacing your rental expenses with ownership. Many argue that you don't have to own your home.

That is very true. But let me shed some enlightenment on that. A doctor may recommend that you need to take more vitamins. Do you have to take vitamins? No; it's a recommendation for your own good.

Recommendations are not mandatory. But you would agree that it is wise to pay attention when a professional or an expert recommends something right? So I recommend that you pay attention here.

While everyone's financial profile doesn't always benefit from home ownership, most people's financial profile will benefit from home ownership for many more reasons starting with these 7.

1. Sense of Ownership
2. Sense of Pride
3. Equity Building
4. Asset Building
5. Credit Building
6. Tax Savings
7. Elevated Purchasing Power

As we go through this book, you will learn more about these individual reasons. But I strongly recommend that you own your personal home because with everything else being equal, it makes the most financial sense.

Two of our most basic needs of life are food and shelter. Either we like it or not, we have to have these things. As a responsible adult in America or any developed country, you live and die by paying for these things.

When you look at most of your other bills such as power, energy, water etc, they are all connected to shelter or housing. Even the healthiest financial profile allocates 25% - 30% of income to housing cost.

For example if you make $5,000 per month, you really shouldn't be spending more than $1,500 on rent or cost of housing (*mortgage principal, interest, taxes and insurance*). Most people don't pay attention to that.

The only exception to that is if you purchase a 2 Family unit home. Since you have another unit that creates income, it's an awesome excuse to take on a bigger mortgage payment. It's just simple arithmetics.

This book is about leveraging real estate to build your overall financial profile. If you made $5,000 per month, you have up to $1,500 that you can spend on housing every month. You now have two choices on how you want to spend that money.

One choice is to spend it as a sunk cost of life; to rent an apartment to live in. The second choice is to have a portion of it going towards the principal of a mortgage loan and another portion towards a tax write-off-able interest.

From a real estate investment standpoint, it's an exit strategy. Therefore you have to make sure it's a profitable exit strategy either in the short term but most importantly in the long term. It's very important to pay particular attention to the value of time against cash.

So let's play around with these numbers. In order to get approved for a conventional mortgage loan, a 20% down payment is typically required. Let's consider a home purchase of $100,000

That means you would need a $20,000 down payment. Most banks will give you $80,000 provided you have an acceptable credit score to complete the purchase. That's not all.

In addition to the $20,000 cash out of pocket, you will need an additional estimated 5% towards closing cost. So in total, you will need to show $25,000 cash in order to purchase a $100,000 home.

If you are a first time buyer who plans to live in the home, that's called "owner occupied." If you are an owner occupied especially first time buyer, there are programs available that require only 5% down payment or less.

In that case, you will only need a total of $10,000 in order to purchase a $100,000 home. These are good numbers so far from a long term stand point. If you can manage to get the mortgage and pay back the loan over time, it's already a profitable exit strategy when you purchase real estate.

But in the short term, what does this mean?

The term of a typical mortgage loan is 30 years. But we need more information to determine if this is a good situation within the next 12 - 60 months. Let's find out.

The idea is to replace your rental expense with an asset building expense. How much will it cost to service the mortgage loan every month?

With a $20,000 down payment, your monthly mortgage at an interest rate of 5% is $425 monthly. At a downpayment of $5,000 as an owner occupied home purchased at $100,000, it will cost $504 per month to service the loan. If you are wondering, "servicing the loan" simply means to make the monthly payment.

That's just the principal and interest. Usually, you will be required to pay property taxes and homeowners insurance. In New Jersey, you can estimate around an additional $1,000 per month in additional obligations when you own a home. Keep in mind that the total housing cost to you will vary.

So to simplify this, you have $510 to pay in principal and interest. Then you have additional $990 to pay in taxes and insurance. Your total expense is $1,500 (P.I.T.I).

P.I.T.I - Principal, Interest, Taxes, Insurance

If you don't buy a home, you would still be paying rent which your landlord pays towards all these 4 expenses. The main one that you are missing out on is the principal.

Paying principal is not a real expense. It builds your equitable interest in real estate. That's what makes it an asset.

The principal is the actual money borrowed for the purchase being paid back over time. However there is a cost for using that money. That's what we refer to as "interest."

Your principal payment in the beginning of the 30 years period is lower. Majority of your mortgage payment goes towards interest in the beginning. But as time goes on, you pay more into your principal and interest lowers.

Here is an example.

With the $510 per month, $114 goes towards principal in the first month while $396 goes towards interest. In layman language, the bank charges you $396 to use $95,000 for the first 30 days.

By the time you finish paying the loan off in 30 years, $508 of the last month's payment goes towards principal to pay off the loan completely. Only $2 goes towards interest.

That means you paid $2 for the use of that $508 in that last 30 days. That is what you call amortization. You pay a little over time to own and build that $100,000 asset. There is also a good chance based on history that the asset will be worth a whole lot more.

What's the alternative? Without this exit strategy, buy and own, you would have spent $1,500 x 12 months x 30 years ($540,0000) on renting. Then at the end of that 30 year period, you do not own the asset.

In certain uncommon scenarios, your overall financial profile doesn't benefit from home ownership. For most people, there are much more benefits, even much more than the seven I gave earlier. It's the first exit strategy you must leverage.

If you have a W2 income, home ownership is one of the best ways to lower your taxable income. The interest you will be paying for the use of all that money is tax deductible.

As a young entrepreneur, the way my income was set up discouraged home ownership. I run a home office, I am able to write off a portion of my rent to lower taxes.

That's not bad but I am missing out on building an asset. About one third of my monthly housing expense could have been going towards building equity in a home; arguably. But those are the facts on what's possible when you leverage this real estate exit strategy.

As an entrepreneur, there are many other ways that I have been able to build long term equity. In fact, writing this book is one of them in all honesty. But nothing is stopping me from leveraging the roof over my head to build even some more equity.

In the next chapter, we will dive into spreading your real estate wings a little further. As I said earlier in this book, passive income, residual income and cash flow is king; not cash.

These numbers work no matter what shape and form you put them in. If they work, it only makes sense to double down. In fact, you have to go all in; don't you think?

CHAPTER 6

Buy & Rent

Beyond buying a home for you and your family to live in, you can start building a portfolio of rental properties one at a time. This is the very first exit strategy that I fell in love with. But it's the one that I am presently not taking enough advantage of, as much as I want to—unfortunately.

Initially, it made sense for me to become a landlord multiple times over. But over the years, I've seen so many horror stories of landlordship. Many people do not realize that being a landlord is, in fact, a full-time endeavor.

Basically, you have to manage people and properties. With that comes liabilities that many are not properly prepared for. If you take on the role of a landlord, you get called for everything wrong at the property.

What's the alternative? There is a distinct difference between being a landlord and being an investor. The former is the only source of rental income while the latter is a liability. But someone has to be the caretaker; it doesn't have to be you.

Most new landlords get excited over very little monthly cash flow without the awareness of the amount of responsibilities involved. Some of this cash flow can be as low as $300 per month. But then every time they turn around, something is broken that will cost $1,500 to fix.

The other day, a friend of mine who purchased a two-family property from another agent gave me a breakdown of the financials. Even though he is one of the few lucky ones with all units rented out, he's found out that he is in deep trouble.

He collects $2,450 in total rent from the property. His total P.I.T.I (principal, interest, taxes, and insurance) payment is $2,175. So on the surface, it seems like he is cash flowing $275, but here is the reality.

About 4 months ago, a few pipes connected to the heating system burst in his basement. It cost him $2,000 upfront to fix. So in reality, he is negatively cash flowing for at least the next 7 months after that event.

In an ideal world, all responsibilities attached to the ownership of the property should also stop. But that's not the case. In fact, for him, more issues have come up since that, costing him more money.

One can claim that it's worth it because owning rental properties is a long-term endeavor. While that is true, short-term losses can send your financial profile into a hole you may not be able to come out of.

It is important to set up your **"buy and rent"** deals for both short and long term success. Doing things based on just long term is synonymous to pure speculation. Speculation is a terrible business and income strategy.

It almost seems impossible to get this right. But it's actually very simple to identify a few criteria and set up rules to protect you and your investment in the short term as well as the long term. The best balance between short and long term happens when you measure your returns and rewards based on an annual basis.

There are a few numbers that I like to look at but they are grouped under these four categories.

1. Cost of Acquisition
2. Annual Expenses
3. Annual Income
4. Annual R.O.I

Let's play around in each of these categories for a simple understanding of why you should pay attention to them.

1: Cost of Acquisition

This category covers the amount of money that it takes you to acquire a piece of property. It would typically include the actual purchase price, estimated cost of repair if it needs work and closing cost.

2: Annual Expenses

These are costs incurred on utility and maintenance of the property over time. Typically, you would use OPM (a mortgage loan) to purchase the property. Therefore, your annual expenses start with the P.I.T.I. (Principal, Interest, Taxes and Insurance).

Most of these expenses come in the form of monthly bills. For each one that comes as monthly bills, you must multiply by 12 months to derive the annual amount. For accurate assessment, the number we care about is the annual total of these expenses.

This is a part that most people skip. Maintenance, repairs and property management will cost money. You must have a conservative estimate of these inevitable expenses ahead of time.

Maintenance is things like lawn and grass cutting, snow plowing and more. Things like these along with property management will cost you at least time. If you value your time like all successful investors do, you will assign an expense amount to these activities.

In all honesty, you should be outsourcing such activity. But I understand you may be on your first property and feel like you have the time. When you set up room for these expenses in your exit strategy, you will at least have that option.

Remember that option is power. Not having these types of options is what positions amateur investors' back against the wall. Part of the **"exit before entry"** strategy is to insure your real estate journey against the inevitable; expensive surprises.

Things will break. A tenant will sometimes need to call someone at 12 midnight for a broken fixture. The idea is for you to have them call someone else unless you are in the property management business.

Most Landlords don't have profitable real estate portfolios. Investors do. Being a landlord involves the full time job of a property manager. Pay someone else for that and include that as part of the expenses.

Property management usually costs around 10-15% of the rental income. That also means that your property manager has invested interest in ensuring 0% vacancy. Speaking of vacancy, you need to include a portion in your expenses for a 10% vacancy factor.

It will happen. Sometimes rental units will sit without being rented out. The longer it takes to get it rented out, the more money leaks through your property finances. Obviously, that would work against your objective.

So sure you may expect a monthly rental roll of $2,450 per month. Let's multiply that by 12 months. That gives us an annual rental income of $29,400.

Most people think of that as a net income. By reading this book, you know better now. One of the most important expenses in thE property financials is the 10% vacancy factor. So 10% of $29,400 equals $2,940 per year.

In addition to that, you have a competent property management cost of another 10% which is $2,940 per year. The difference remaining after deducting these two important costs is $23,520 ($29,400 - $2,940 - $2,940).

Property managers make their money from the rental income. That also means that they have invested interest in 0% vacancy. So it serves you multi-dimensionally to hire a property manager.

Let's take this a step further. Add another 10% towards maintenance and repair. So even if you never spend this money, the money stays in the property's designated bank account.

Every property comes with utility bills for services such as power supply, water, gas, sewage, homeowners association fees etc. I suggest estimating about 20% for these real expenses. For the example above, that will be $5,880 per year which is $490 per month.

Any units that have separate meters for some of these utility services will save you money. That gives you an opportunity to pass that payment obligation over to the tenants. But you will still be responsible for the common areas such as hallways, exterior and basements.

Ideally, you should have at least 10% in cash on cash returns per year. We will cover that part under the income category. For now, let's go over these expenses.

- Utility Services (20%)
- Property Management (10%)
- Maintenance and Repair (10%)
- Vacancy Factor (10%)
- Mortgage (P.I.T.I)

Those percentages are all estimates and can be moved to suit your needs. The idea is to give you the knowledge and the tool to design your buy and rent exit strategy for profits. As you can imagine, most people just dive into it with blindfolds on.

I had to take this time to demonstrate how important it is to pre-plan these expenses. Expenses get very expensive when you don't account for them upfront. That's especially true in the "Buy and Rent" exit strategy.

3: Annual Income

This may seem like the fun part but this is the first step to most landlords' downfall. It's very easy to over speculate in this category. There is nothing wrong with being optimistic but this is not the category where you want to do that.

Typically, you will see a range of potential rental rates here and there. For example in Newark, New Jersey, you will see a range of $900-$1,400 for a 2 bedroom apartment. Most aspiring landlords will calculate their potential profits based on the higher end of that range.

If you want to do that, you might as well go to a religious house to pray for money to fall out of the sky. That's not a very smart thing to do. The only way to ensure capitalizing on the higher end of potential profit range is by adding value to the property. Hoping that you will be lucky is a terrible strategy.

4: Annual R.O.I

There are 2 types of return on investment (R.O.I) that are available to look at in your financials. One is the overall R.O.I with respect to the total cost of acquisition including other people's money (OPM). The other ROI is called cash on cash which is calculated with respect to the actual money out of your pocket (i.e not including OPM).

Personally, I am only interested in the cash on cash return because it's the number that shows my true ability to flip money. However note that the banks are interested in the overall ROI as it reveals the return on their part of the investment. It's also the number that assures them security in the investment into your deals.

When you pay attention to these number categories, you are automatically ahead of 90% of the game. Doesn't that make you feel safe? With these methods, your portfolio will be air tight.

You can even break one or two rules and be okay. The idea is awareness of these loopholes. This knowledge and wisdom give you the tools to fill them as you collect passive and residual income while building equity.

As you build the equity, you can flip it to more cash and do it over and over again. It may seem hard to find this types of deals but it isn't. That's why we are here to help you.

In the next chapter, I will share with you one of the methods that we use to find these deals. Fortunately, it's also a very lucrative exit strategy all by itself. But in combination with 'buy and rent', you become one of the kings and queens in the game.

CHAPTER 7

Wholesaling & Short Sales

It remains a fact that the more value you add to real estate, the more money gets added to your net worth. The more difficult it seems to create a deal, the more value you can add. Therefore, some of the most lucrative exit strategies involve acquiring properties from negative equity owners.

So one day, I received a call from one of my advertisements to distressed homeowners. His name was Carlos. He needed to get rid of the property as far back as 3 years ago. But it seemed impossible.

In a typical situation, he decided to pay for an appraisal to determine the fair market value of the property. The appraisal report came back at a value of $220,000. The property is worth $220,000 as derived from a thorough analysis of 6 months of recent sales of properties within a mile radius from the subject property.

Unfortunately, he had paid $375,000 for the property 2 years prior to that. It's a 2 Family unit property. He lived in one of the units until a sudden call to transfer to another state by his job.

He put down a 3.5% down payment on the home, and the bank gave him the rest of the money. The original principal loan balance was $361,875. After 2 years of consistently paying the monthly mortgage payment of $1,943, the remaining principal balance was $350,443.

With taxes and insurance, his total monthly payment was about $3,100 per month. He was able to rent out the 2nd unit after 5 months of purchasing the property. So in addition to the initial $20,000 that he spent on down payment and closing costs, he has spent an additional $16,000+ on upkeep of the property.

At that point, he was stressed out with the idea of being a landlord. That dream has been shattered, and it took his bank account balance for a nosedive as well. So by the time he found a tenant for the 2nd unit, he was ready to offload the property.

He was able to rent the unit at $1,250. The agent who sold him the property had assured him that he could get $1,800 per month for the unit. He decided to settle for the $1,250 after having the apartment sit vacant for 5 months.

Anyway, that left him with a monthly obligation of $1,850. It was a bit relieving to have that apartment rented out. He thought he, at least, had a job to cover his bills. If he was renting, he would be renting the same size of his side of the building for about $1,250 - $1,350.

Well, he thought it's still not bad as he is paying down his mortgage balance and building equity. He was also able to write off interest paid to lower his taxable income. Everything seemed okay until he got the message from his job for a mandatory transfer to another state.

He was left with not many conventional choices. Remember that he owed $350,000 and stuck with $3,100 total monthly and mandatory expenses. He had to move.

If he didn't move, he would lose the only source of income that had allowed him to sustain so far in the middle of that financial hole. He moved to his new job role.

Again, the apartment was standing vacant for another 3 months before he could rent it out. So he rented out the apartment at $1,300. His rent roll was now a total of $2,550.

So even though he had moved, he had to keep paying an extra $550 out of pocket to maintain servicing the loan. His bank account went negative and overdraft every other month. He was stressed out and it affected his marriage as well.

Finally, he stopped paying on the property altogether. One month later, one of his tenants moved out. That's when he decided to find out what the property is worth to list it for sale at a fair market value.

So he found out it was worth $220,000. His principal balance at that point was $350,000. So he had a negative equity of $130,000 in the property after 2 years. That would mean he has to come up with $130,000 in personal cash to sell; technically.

Three months after he stopped payment, he received an intention to foreclose/pending lawsuit notification from the court. He felt so sad and stuck until he responded to one of my advertisements that says "WE BUY HOUSES, NEGATIVE EQUITY, NO PROBLEM."

When he called, I offered him $130,000 for the property. I came up with that offer by multiplying its value ($220,000) by 65% and then subtracting a repair estimate of $10,000.

He asked me how that would be possible since he would have to pay an additional $220,000 to pay off the $350,000 balance on the mortgage. Then I explained the short sale method to him and why the bank allows it.

You see the bank is not in the business of managing properties. They are in the business of multiplying money. But when money stops coming in from a mortgage payment, the mortgage is now referred to as a non-performing asset.

At that point, the $350,000 balance is assumed to be non-existent, and all that matters is whatever they can get from the fair market value of the property. In fact and reality, the $350,000 mortgage note is not worth the original value.

But practically accepting my $130,000 offer is better than the mortgage payment of $1,943 that is no longer coming in. Remember that Carlos had already stopped payment for the property for more than one year.

This is called a short sale. The only usual stipulation or condition on a short sale approval is that the bank doesn't want the seller to get any money from the sales proceeds. That usually makes sense to the seller. They are more than happy since the bank will not be holding them for the balance before they can offload a non-performing asset.

A short sale is a great way to buy properties at a discount. Most mortgage banks will order a broker's price opinion (BPO) on the property to determine if your offer is within a certain range. Once an agent calls to do the BPO, present them with a copy of your justification for your low offer.

Your justification can include repair estimates and comparable sales. The agent usually takes these things into consideration when reporting an official opinion of value to the bank.

Many banks automatically accept any offer more than 90% of the property's fair market value. With proper negotiation skills, anything is possible.

Carlos was underwater with his property. He owed more than the property was worth. So the only way he could sell it was to get a short sale approval to replace the full payoff.

If not, the closing agent and/or title company will detect a $350,000 lien that needed to be paid off. A sale price of $220,000 or lower would not be enough, and the sale will not close.

So what I did was agree to $140,000 after a counteroffer from the bank. Then I sold the approval contract to an end buyer for $25,000. So the total purchase price to the end buyer is ($140,000 + $25,000) $165,000.

This exit strategy is called wholesaling. My end buyer is happy because they purchased a $220,000 property at $165,000. That's a $55,000 discount.

Don't forget that the same property value was at $350,000 at the height of the market when Carlos purchased it.

It's a win-win strategy. But it takes some work, starting with marketing to distressed homeowners. I was able to create lots of lucrative deals like this because of the magnitude of value created.

It creates peace of mind for the seller, and the end buyer gets to secure quality properties at discounts.

The mortgage bank also gets to recoup some lost money for the bank. If you, as the facilitator of this deal, didn't step in, the bank may foreclose at some point after losing 2 different ways.

They would have lost more time (which is worth more than money itself) and get a lot less than $140,000. In addition to that, most abandoned homes from stressed-out or accidental landlords get vandalized.

In many other cases, the seller will have other reasons for desperate needs to offload a property outside of negative equity. Many vacant homes are owned free and clear. Some of them are unwanted inheritances.

There would be no need for Short Sales when the owner doesn't owe as much as a property is worth. All you have to do is get the property under contract using the same formula (65% of its After Repair Value ARV) and wholesale the contract by assigning it to an end buyer for a fee.

That's wholesaling. The strategy falls under massive and not passive income as you only get paid that one time.

The minimum target fee for you to walk away with in wholesaling is $10,000. The highest I have made from this strategy is $82,000 from one deal.

You don't need cash outside of marketing expenses to capitalize on this strategy. You don't need a good credit score as you will not be the end buyer. All you need is this knowledge you are acquiring right now and people to help offload unwanted properties.

If you choose this strategy to make money from real estate, your primary responsibility and input is marketing. Your job is to create marketing to find motivated sellers and build an end buyer's list and/or network. I cover this in detail in my published book Smart Real Estate Wholesaling, which you can find at www.SmartRealEstateWholesaling.com

The most common ways to find wholesale deals are:

1. **Driving for dollars** - which means driving around town looking for vacant houses.
2. **Cold calling** - skip tracing owners for potential candidate properties and calling them.

3. **Direct mailing** - sending letters to purchased list of public records such as preforeclosures, tax delinquency etc
4. **Street bandit signs** - hanging signs on electric poles that say "we buy houses".
5. **Door knocking** properties on any of these lists

In my humble opinion, all 5 of these strategies are old school simply because it does not involve the best use of your time and resources. Internet marketing provides an opportunity for a lot cheaper and more efficient ways to market today. As I said earlier, I covered that in a lot more details in my book, Smart Real Estate Wholesaling, which you can find at www.SmartRealEstateWholesaling.com

In the next chapter, we will get into getting paid for fixing the neighborhoods. If you are more of the handy type unlike me, this is an awesome way to get massive money from real estate. You can also add passive income cheaply to your portfolio.

Let's keep it moving.

CHAPTER 8

Buy, Fix & Flip

If you are the handy type, this exit strategy is probably the one you will enjoy the most. When you enjoy the process, your chances of a profitable investing journey skyrockets.

It flows all the way through from acquisition to closing of the exit transaction because it's just that much fun. As you already know, the more value you add, the more profits you make. The energy you bring into the project through your passion for handy work will translate to profits.

In a **fix and flip** deal, two closings will be encountered. One closing happens for acquisition while the other closing happens for the exit. After the exit closing is when you can determine if you made profit or not.

So it goes like this. You find a property that needs work. The first step is to determine what it is worth after repair. As a refresher, that's called "after repair value" or A.R.V. The next step is to determine the repair cost estimate.

Here is an example.

A seller calls you from your *"we buy houses"* advertising and needs to get rid of a house he inherited a few years back. He has since refinanced and pulled money out of the equity, but he still wants $5,000 cash to walk away. After filling out your lead sheet and questionnaire, you have the following information.

1st Step (ARV) = $300,000

Repair Cost Estimate (RCE) = $35,000

These are the two pieces of information that you need to make an offer. In order to calculate the maximum allowable offer (MAO), multiply the ARV by 65% and deduct the RCE. Let's do it.

MAO = (ARV x 65%) - RCE

MAO = ($300,000 x 65%) - $35,000

MAO = $195,000 - $35,000

MAO = $160,000

So the maximum allowable offer will be $160,000 to purchase this deal in a way that allows you to add value for profits. Some other gurus will advice to use 70% as opposed to 65%. I like 65% because it leaves you room for negotiations.

If you want to leave room for a 2nd possible exit strategy such as wholesaling to other investors, 65% is definitely a better way to scale your exit. I definitely recommend having a back up exit strategy structured in.

When you offer $160,000, the seller may counter offer you with $170,000. Let's use 70% to determine if that's still within our offer range.

MAO = (ARV x **70%**) - RCE

MAO = ($300,000 x **70%**) - $35,000

MAO = $210,000 - $35,000

MAO = $175,000

So you actually have a $15,000 offer range. However the closer you get to the higher end of that range, the more you will be restricted to "fix and flip" as an exit strategy. Also, the lower the fees you can make on the deal as a wholesaler.

Anyway this chapter is about fix and flip. Let's focus on that. Just remember that backup exit strategies are highly recommended.

In this case, this seller only wanted $5,000. According to the lead sheet and questionnaire, he has 2 liens against the property. There is a first mortgage of $123,000 and second position lien of $35,000.

That's a total of $163,000 debt that has to be satisfied in order to acquire the property. You got the funds together and acquired the property at a closing in 15 days. That's the entry closing but now it's time to add value to the property so that you can exit with a potential profit. What's the potential profit here?

Cost of Acquisition (COA) = $163,000

RCE = $35,000

ARV = $300,000

Potential Profit (PP) = ARV - COA - RCE

= $300,000 - $163,000 - $35,000

'Gross' Potential Profit (PP) = $102,000

That's a pretty nice payday right? But I have to keep it one 'hunnid' (100%) with you. There are two types of costs that haven't been accounted for in the example above.

- Holding cost
- Closing cost

Holding cost is the cost you will incur between your entry and exit closing. We already know the repair cost estimate for the fix/rehab project. But there will be utilities and possible financing costs incurred as well.

I suggest that you factor in 5% of the ARV as an estimate for holding cost. That will be $15,000 potentially less your gross projected profit of $102,000; still left with $87,000.

Closing cost may be incurred twice because there may be two closings from acquisition to exit closing. I suggest that you also factor another 5% of the ARV ($15,000). There is a very high chance that you will not use all that money but it's better to be prepared than to be sorry.

What is the total cost of the project (TCP)? We have to account for the cost of acquisition, repair cost estimate, holding cost and closing cost.

That will be:

$163,000 + $35,000 + $15,000 + $15,000

TCP = $228,000

So potentially, you can spend 60-90 days on this rehab project and make a net profit (NP) of $72,000. Do you think that's a healthy ROI (return on investment)?

ROI = (NP/TCP) x 100

= ($72,000/$228,000) x 100

Projected ROI = 31.6%

The ROI that we need to call this a good deal is 30%. The example that we just went through beat it. Once you estimate a deal and it projects a minimum of 30% ROI in projected TCP, lock it in and you are about to get paid.

One of my favorite and most simple fix and flip deals are "ADD A LEVEL". This involves purchasing the old school cape cod style homes with an attic. Then adding a second level to give it more square footage.

Most of the cape cods are 2 bedroom and 1 bathroom houses; at least here in New Jersey. When you add a full second floor, you are able to add a third and masters bedroom with another full bathroom. You can also add a half guest toilet on the first floor by the living room.

That makes the home a 4 bedroom, 2 and half bathroom. With a new kitchen, appliances and finished basement, you will turn a $170,000 cape cod home to a $600,000 home in central New Jersey. That's a prime example of turning value to massive income.

COA = $170,000

REC = $150,000

TCP = $370,000

ARV = $600,000

Project Net Profit = $230,000

Project R.O.I = 38%; a whole lot more than our desired 30%. Note that you may not even be using your personal cash for these deals. Therefore the true cash-on-cash return on investment is a whole lot more. But you can at least get your cash partners 8-12% return on their money.

There are 5 more questions we need to answer to give this chapter proper justice within the scope of this book.

- How do you fund a fix and flip deal once you find a potential 30% ROI?
- Should you do some work by yourself during the rehab like you see on HGTV shows?
- How do you avoid getting duped by contractors during the rehab project?
- Should you go big or start small?
- What happens if you finish rehab and can't sell quickly?

Let's get to answering…

How do you fund a fix and flip deal once you find a potential 30% ROI? As usual, my favorite way is to use OPM (other people's money). It increases your purchase and leverage power.

The only exception to that rule is if you are not involved in the rehab and all you are doing is acting like a bank. If that's what you are doing, you simply want to make sure that you are doing your due diligence on the people you are lending to; credit ratings, personal guarantees and all.

If you are reading this book, I am assuming that you don't have millions to throw into deals you are not monitoring personally. You are in this because you want to be involved in the project. As you know, you are either investing from a time standpoint or money standpoint.

Let the banks and lenders fund the deals while you focus on the project. Leverage their money to make returns on their money and simultaneously feed your bank account. The interest and other costs of using OPM is already factored in the estimates I illustrated earlier.

Here are four viable funding sources for you to research to fund your deals:

- Hard money lending
- 203K for owner occupied only

- Private lending
- Joint venture partnerships

Be mindful that most of them still need personal guarantors with good credit especially if you do not have any experience in fix and flips. Once you get in the door with 2 or 3 successful projects, it's really all about relationships. It becomes easier to fund all the deals you can handle.

You may have family and friends who have cash in the bank laying around too. That's when you use the joint venture partnership method.

Just be mindful of having a well structured and written agreement on what everyone brings to the table and expected returns and reward. People can be mad (as in crazy) and have a tendency to have amnesia when you partner with them. Be clear that there are no guarantees; in written form. However, investments are backed with real estate and real assets.

Should you do some work by yourself during the rehab like you see on HGTV shows? That is the worst idea ever. On TV, it looks so cool until you get into major issues where contractors will then charge you more to fix your mess.

I suggest that you use professionals and people that fix properties for a living. You cannot afford to treat "fix and flips" like a hobby. Treat it like a real business and it will pay you like a real business.

After all, it's all about making the numbers work as I illustrated earlier. Once you hire the right people, you can then get involved to help them. There is too much money and a lot at risk to be practicing with.

How do you avoid getting duped by contractors during the rehab project? Don't pay out all the money at once. Limit all disbursements of funds to a few thousand dollars at a time. Divide the project to a minimum of four phases and even sub-phases (a.k.a segments based on deliverables) and job completion with clear expected time of completion for each sub-phase.

Don't pay out funds and/or move on to the next segment unless the present segment is completed. If a segment of the project is completed late, collect a reason and document it. If a segment is completed earlier than scheduled, create an incentive for early completion.

Motivation is your responsibility. It also encourages the contractor to feel like they are on your team. The incentive will automatically serve as the punishment for late completion. Punishments can also include terminating the whole project contract for repeated incomplete segments and phases.

Should you go big or start small? I strongly suggest starting small. In fact, if you see an opportunity to start in partnerships with others, it will only equip you. You can also use it to leverage other people's mistakes and experiences. (OPM & OPE).

What happens if you finish rehab and can't sell quickly? You need to partner with a good agent and invest in staging. Staging is the process of furnishing the home to look like someone already lives there.

The idea is to make potential buyers dream about your property as a home. You need their emotions to be engaged. People buy with their emotions 85% of the time and justify with logic later.

Engaging your potential buyers' emotions is your responsibility. There will be no profits unless the 2nd and exit closing in the project happens. That's why it's buy, fix and flip.

CHAPTER 9

Buy, Fix & Rent

The whole point of getting into real estate investing is to build wealth… right? Well there is no such thing as building wealth without passive and residual income. It's even better when you can get into the rental properties with some inbuilt equity.

What is equity?

Equity is the amount of actual ownership that you've actually built into a property. For example, imagine that you own a property with an appraised value of $100,000 but you owe a total debt of $75,000 against the property. In that case, you have an equity of $25,000 ($100,000 - $75,000).

Typically, it takes time as you pay monthly on your liens such as mortgages and line of credit to build equity. When you purchase a property with a mortgage financing, you start with small to zero equity. As you start making your payments over time, you build equity.

As shown earlier in mortgage amortization examples, more of your monthly mortgage payment goes towards interest in the beginning. As you get closer towards the end of the mortgage term (typically 30 years), more of the same monthly payment goes towards paying off the principal loan balance. The more you pay off the principal balance, the more equity you build into the ownership with respect to present market valuation of the property.

What is inbuilt equity?

Imagine buying a property that is worth $100,000 in today's market at a purchase price of $75,000. That gets you into the ownership with an inbuilt equity of $25,000. On a typical deal, it will take you about 10 - 12 years to build that amount of equity.

One thing that's worth a whole lot more than money is time. With "buy, fix and rent", you can use the 'fix' aspect to add value that will replace time therefore entering into ownership with pre-built or inbuilt-equity.

There are a few ways to build equity in general. Obviously, the most popular way is to buy a property at fair market value. Then you pay your regular mortgage payment over time. With the exit strategy discussed in this chapter, you can maximize your bottom line further.

Previously, we covered "buy, fix and flip" AND "buy, fix and own." How you find these deals are basically the same. The only difference here is the very extreme end of the exit which is renting.

Instead of leveraging your housing expense for building equity, you simply set this exit up towards passive and residual income from rental properties. In the case of buy, fix and flip, you retain fixed up properties with inbuilt or prebuilt equity for fast massive profits.

- Step 1: Buy a fixer upper property.
- Step 2: Fix/Rehab the property to rentable condition.

- Step 3: Rent it out to tenants.

The only downside for most investors that use this exit is the fact that they have to manage rehab projects as well as manage people in the form of tenants. Those two things are separate full time endeavors. Therefore you need a well oiled operation to pull this off.

Well oiled operation is not synonymous to hiring multiple employees. It's not about the size of your operation. It's really more about your project management and people skills. You will find partnerships and collaborations quite useful.

In my first 2 years in real estate, I received and loved the nice $30,000 checks. But I found out within 3 years that they only lasted for so long. The market crashed on its face and my business crashed along with it.

I had no cash flow to fall back on. It was a scary moment in business because I could not think straight as my lifestyle bills chased me down to overdrafted bank accounts eventually. That's not a fun place to find yourself especially after tasting success beyond the average.

Therefore rental income is the best exit strategy as you get to build an income and cash flow portfolio. It also spreads your liability across multiple dimensions. In default, you build equity over time as opposed to building bills when you get used to massive house flipping checks.

But just buying rental properties are often not good enough to maximize gains in certain markets. In hot markets, the value of properties are partly influenced by rental value while other parts are influenced by retail, emotions and fair market value.

For example, you can walk into Newark New Jersey right now and pick up a two family unit for $350,000. With a 3.5% down payment ($12,250), that monthly payment (P.I.T.I) will be about $2,900.

In order for you to break even on just that payment, you need each unit to command a rental income of $1,450 each. That's basically pushing the higher end of the rental market in Newark. It's highly unlikely that you will get $1,450 for a 2 bedroom apartment in that area.

The average rent in that area ranges from $875 - $1,250. On top of that, there are other expenses, right? Remember these expenses.

- Utility Services (20%)
- Property Management (10%)
- Maintenance and Repair (10%)
- Vacancy Factor (10%)
- And...Mortgage (P.I.T.I)

You need room in your exit estimates to create your profits ahead of entry. In these hot markets, it's harder to buy a rental property at fair market value and create instant cash flow.

As you can see, $2,900 is required for at least 50% of the income that this property needs to produce in order to cash flow at the desired ROI. If you are marketing to a lot of distressed owners with high equity, you can "buy and rent" with immediate cash flow. It's very hard to find these types of profitable deals from the open market such as the MLS.

However there are tons of deals on the open market that need work. They are called fixer-uppers or TLC (tender loving care). Because they need work, they are typically priced significantly below the market value.

For example, that $350,000 property is sold for that much at market value because it was already fully renovated. Imagine an identical property just a few houses down the block but needing $60,000 renovation.

With simple math, it should be listed at $290,000 ($350,000 - $60,000) right? It doesn't work like that. Such property would probably be listed for sale at $200,000 or less.

It's less desirable so it's listed significantly lower in order to attract sales faster. Emotions are less of a factor for a potential buyer, therefore the numbers need to attract the buyer such as you, the investor, who will add value for the purpose of creating massive profits.

These types of properties are ideal candidates for inbuilt equity and cash flow in hot markets where properties get very pricey based on demand. So if you paid $200,000 for the house and rehab it for an additional $60,000, your total cost will be $260,000.

You just saved $90,000. By saving $90,000, what does that mean in cash flow for your rental investment? That's $600 more than what it would have been. There are other parts of your expenses that will drop just for saving that money on your total cost of acquisition and rehab.

When you use the "buy, rent and fix" as an exit strategy over a number of properties, it can also have a compound effect on your overall financial profile. On a 5th house, you could have increased your monthly rental cash flow by $3,000 (5 x $600) but that's not it.

With everything else being equal, you've also added $1.75 million worth of assets to your financial profile. Here is the best part. If you set it up with the path I revealed to you in chapter 6, you will have tenants paying down all the lien and loans against these assets without the typical responsibilities of a landlord.

Remember investors make money while landlords end up struggling. Investors visit the bank and landlords patrol eviction courts. Are you seeing the picture here?

As an investor, you also have a backup exit strategy. You could have easily turned around and decided to wholesale that property to a retail buyer for a net profit of $90,000. You can rent it and you can flip it. You have options.

So this is one of my favorite exit strategies that involves an actual deed closing and transfer. It's also the last that I will cover in this book. Just realize that I left the best for last.

Have you heard of the B.R.R.R.R strategy? It stands for buy, rehab, rent, refinance and repeat. It's basically repeating the strategy in this chapter over and over again in order to build millions of dollars in net worth.

It also allows you to leverage the equity on each subsequent property(ies) as down payment for the next. It's "scaling your real estate empire" on steroids.

I would definitely revisit this chapter and chapter 6 over and over again if I were you. Most especially, I love it because it presents opportunities for both passive and massive income.

If you ever want to take it a step further, you can help your friends, family, associates and acquaintances facilitate "buy, fix and rent" while building a million dollar property management business system from it.

In the next few chapters, we want to dive into some non-conventional ways to make money from real estate instruments. The universal truth around the world is that real estate is the ultimate money and investment vehicle. Even Wall Street can't argue with that.

While it's cute to buy and sell real estate, let's talk about the power behind the instruments that drove the

American economy way up so fast and it crashed. It crashed so much that it caused a global recession.

With that kind of financial impact, you would agree that an unusual level of market confidence has been created. So how can you tap into this level of confidence to build your financial profile? That's the question to be answered next.

These are not necessarily my favorite exit strategies but they work because the world truly believes in real estate. It's the most powerful investment vehicle. The good news is that it's also the most easily accessible vehicle for an average person.

The strategies we are about to discuss in the next chapter are not my most favorite strategies because of potential exposure to legal problems. Nonetheless, real estate is powerful enough to drive money through some very creative strategies. I want to share them with you.

CHAPTER 10

Subject To & Rent to Own

Imagine acquiring a property without inheriting responsibility for liens or mortgages against it. Do these responsibilities disappear after the transfer of deeds? No.

In fact it stays with the property. So we need a motive to take over a property "subject to" existing liens and mortgages against the property. Why would you want to buy a property subject to an existing mortgage?

Oftentimes, a straight real estate acquisition is not feasible. The numbers just would not work out when you make an offer at 65-70% of the after repair value minus the estimated cost of repair. When that happens (the numbers not working out), it doesn't have to be the end of the road.

Let's walk through an example together. A seller has just called you because she needs to get rid of a property. As usual, you grab your new lead sheet to complete with necessary information.

Among many other pieces of vital information, the new lead sheet helps you collect what the property is worth, how much repair it needs and the mortgage owed against the property presently. In addition to that, we also have the monthly mortgage payment (PITI).

Let's break it down.

- Property Value = $400,000
- Repair Estimate = $35,000
- Principal Balance =$250,000
- Monthly Payment (PITI) = $2,650

The mortgage principal balance is presently $250,000 but the original mortgage was $320,000 which was obtained 11 years ago. That means that she has already made 132 monthly payments (11 of 30 years). The original mortgage determines the monthly mortgage payment that your acquisition is "subject to". So what is "subject to"?

"Subject to acquisitions" is the process of purchasing a real estate property while acquiring the responsibility of the existing monthly mortgage payment on the property. Typically, your offer on this property would be $225,000 which is 65% of $400,000 (the after repair value) minus $35,000 repair estimate. But she owes

$250,000 so it's not feasible without a short sale approval as discussed in chapter 7.

But there is a downside to short sales that some like to avoid. With short sales, the seller agrees to sell the house at $225,000 which is less than what is owed to the mortgage bank. She owes $250,000, significantly less than what it is worth after repair; $400,000.

Without selling, the seller would be sitting on $150,000 ($400,000 - $250,000) worth of equity. If she gets the mortgage to agree to short sell at $225,000, the bank will write-off the difference of $25,000. But they will also report it to the federal internal revenue services as taxable income.

That's not a desirable outcome for a seller who cares. Also for the bank to consider short sales, they often require being late on the mortgage payments. There are a couple of disadvantages to late payments as you can imagine.

It stamps the owners credit rating negatively for obvious reasons. When a payment is late for 30 days, it gets stamped; also at 60 and 90 days. That's the first disadvantage of an average short sale process and approval.

Being late on the payment is a required indicator or motivation for the bank to accept a short payoff on the mortgage. Secondly, it's simply not a productive thing to let a mortgage that has been in good standing for 11 years go delinquent.

The seller needs to sell as-off yesterday; fast. You want to buy the property but your offer can't pay off the $250,000 owed presently. At this stage, there is just one more thing to check.

It's not so important to pay off the $250,000. What's more important is to keep the mortgage current. In fact, the owner is only looking to sell because of the stress of the monthly payment required to service the mortgage loan.

We found out earlier that it cost $2,650 to service the mortgage. We also know from chapter 6 that you should pre-plan for double that amount in cash flow, in order to have a healthy and profitable rental property. Let's assume that there are no taxes or other expenses in order to keep it simple for this example.

So in subject to deals, it's all about the terms. The terms are negotiable. In this example deal, the stress of ownership for the seller is that $2,650 monthly payment.

You have decided to acquire the property at a payment of $5,000 "subject to" existing mortgage. That means the deed will be transferred to you. However you will be responsible to pay $2,650 every month for the rest of the mortgage term which is another 19 years.

Why would you want to take over this property with a $2,650 monthly obligation? Let's see.

What if you take over this property and can get it producing $5,000 per month? Obviously, you would want to do that over and over again. That's $2,350 in monthly cash flow; again, assuming no obligation for other expenses.

As usual, the real returns are calculated annually. In this case, the deal is cash flowing $28,200 annually. With an initial investment of $5,000, that comes out to an annualized R.O.I return on investment of 564%.

You relieve the owner of the stressful ownership. You put the property to work. That creates income because you added value to a distressed owner and the community.

Many people don't realize that property ownership is only useful when you make it productive. If you inherit a property free and clear, you can still lose it to foreclosure. Property taxes will never be paid off on a property because the police power only encourages "productive ownership."

So as a real estate investor, you are rewarded for putting properties to work. The tax revenue is obviously part of the revenue stream for the city. This is often a difficult thing for the folks who live in third world countries to figure out.

In third world countries, you can buy land, build a house on it and never owe another dime in taxes ever again. In a developed country, sure you can inherit a property but it has to produce so that taxes can get paid.

So many owners may not have the bandwidth to maintain ownership of a property. That can become a burden on productivity of the property. Weeds may become overgrown and attract code violation tickets.

If enough of those things happen, you may get a call from a distressed owner who needs to offload a potentially productive and profitable property. Get ready to take over.

Now you know that you can even take over the payment obligations provided that you can make the property produce more. With an understanding of this concept, you can take over properties all day long to rent.

The only potential downside is that the existing mortgage bank can exercise the "due on sale" clause rights if they find out that the deed has been transferred to another person. What that means is that they can ask that all $250,000 be paid off immediately if they find out she sold the house. Typically, it doesn't happen if payments continue as usual.

If payment stops, that gives the bank a reason to want money. If money is coming in, there is no reason for them to cry over anything. It's all about the Benjamins.

One of the best add-on exit strategies for this is "rent to own". There are many candidates who will gladly pay you a nice downpayment for rent to own. For one reason or the other, they don't qualify to buy a home the conventional way.

- Bad credit
- Low down payment
- Can't afford closing cost
- Low income

You can offer such a candidate ownership opportunity with an option to purchase the property in the future at predetermined terms. Here is an example:

Stella wants to buy a home now because her lease is up. Her credit score is 476 which is below average but she's got a great job. Instead of waiting to fix her credit, she wants to start experiencing the dream of homeownership right now.

She can afford to put a downpayment of $10,000 into the deal. You agree to apply it towards purchase if she qualifies for a mortgage in 24 months. She will pay a monthly rent of $4,000 monthly until she buys at a predetermined purchase price of $350,000.

So you decided to pass her the opportunity. Among the many benefits of "rent to own" for investors is the fact that you can completely avoid landlord responsibilities. Here are some more benefits.

- Rent to own tenants tend to take over maintenance of the property.
- The down payment is usually larger than your typical security deposit.

- You keep the down payment but the security deposit is legally not yours.
- The monthly rent is usually more than the going rent market rate.
- You get to give someone the dream of homeownership.

Also, you will be selling the property to the tenant in 24 months at $350,000 minus the initial down payment of $10,000. That's equal to $340,000. The original owner of the property owes $250,000 which is probably lower since payments have been current for 24 months.

Let's calculate some profits:

$340,000 minus $250,000 = $90,000 in potential gross profits that you can choose to split with the original owner or not. It all depends on the term that you negotiated but there is serious money to be made.

If you want, you can also link the tenant with a referral to a credit repair to help them qualify for the purchase in 24 months or whatever the term of the "rent to own" contract lasts for. The monthly cash flow tends to be more consistent.

You can even add a stipulation that put the *"lease with option to own"* contract at default risk if they default on payment.

In the next chapter, I have one more unconventional exit strategy to share with you. Just like this strategy, you can make more money while you avoid typical responsibility of homeownership and/or landlordship.

See you in chapter 11.

CHAPTER 11

Mortgage Notes

As you are probably realizing, real estate is such a trustworthy asset class, so many investment opportunities have been created through it. One of the most commonly overlooked ones are mortgage notes. This is bread and butter for the banks.

Most residential real estate property acquisitions are financed by mortgage loans. Every time a mortgage loan is originated, a relationship is *"originated"* between a mortgagor and a mortgagee. So which one is which?

The person getting the loan is the one creating the mortgage note. That's the mortgagor, if you will. The lender is the mortgagee since they are the one receiving the promissory note.

Yes. It's a promissory note that is secured by real estate. The document agreement created when a mortgage is originated contains a promissory note enforceable if the loan defaults.

The promissory note carries the weight and value of the principal balance. But that's just the face value. There is a part of the actual value that accounts for the market value of the note.

With or without control of the real estate asset, the promissory note can be bought, sold and traded. Whoever is in possession of the promissory note has the rights to payments due on the loan per the original promissory note.

When you get calls from collection agencies, have you ever noticed that it is another company entirely? It's because these accounts (aka the promissory notes) get sold at pennies on the dollar to companies who capitalize on them.

For example, if you terminate a Verizon wireless account with an outstanding bill of $400, they may send you reminders for up to 90 days. But after that, your account is considered a non-performing account. In the case of a mortgage, it's considered a non-performing asset.

At this point, the promissory note owner would exercise rights that allow them to create some liquidity. They may sell the $400 promissory note for as low as $40. The idea is to collect $40 in real cash in exchange for paper that's hopefully worth $400; keyword being "hopefully".

Many companies go out of business; not necessarily because of lack of business, but lack of liquidity. Liquidity is the measure of cash flow and cash availability within an operational system.

Continuous flow of new business is key to business survival. This is especially true in this unpredictable and technology driven business environment.

So in efforts to keep money flowing through the banks, mortgage companies are more in the business of promissory notes than they are in the real estate business. If all you had is $10 million to lend out to home buyers, that money will finish at some point.

Let's assume there is a new development and each of the homes cost $500,000. By the time 20 homes are sold, all $10 million is lent out. So does that mean that you are now out of business?

No. It means that your lending business has ran out of liquidity. It's time to create liquidity by selling those $10 million worth of promissory notes.

Are they actually worth $10 million?

It depends on how current the mortgage payments are. If a mortgage is defaulted; meaning that the mortgagor/borrower stops paying on it, it loses value. Think about it; it makes sense right?

An instrument is called an asset based on its ability to produce income. If it can't produce income, it's a liability. So if a promissory note stops creating income for the holder, it becomes less of an asset and more of a liability. It loses its value.

So the note is worth much more than $10 million at his origination and can be sold for more. A $10 million note at the end of 30 years would have generated $9 million in interest from bringing in $50,000 on a monthly basis at 5% annually.

Investors are willing to pay for these types of assets all day long. However, a defaulted mortgage will sell for a lot less than its principal balance. Sometimes, it's better for the mortgagor or lender to sell it in order to move money into other asset classes.

The money you get now is much more valuable than a promissory note that's generating no monthly payment. In addition to that, collection agencies and certain types of loan servicing companies specialize in collecting from defaulted loan borrowers.

How does that work? Imagine a $300,000 promissory note that an investor was trying to get rid off. The note originated at $500,000 with $2,586 monthly payment.

After 18 years of up to date payments, it defaulted at a principal balance of $300,000. There was no longer monthly payment coming in any longer.

So the mortgagee realized that she had collected more than $600,000 in payments. Do the math; $2,685 per month x 12 months x 18 years = $579,960. That's a profit of $79,960.

So the mortgage note was sold for $150,000 to an investor. The collateral property is worth $450,000 at the moment. So that puts the new note owners in a position where they can foreclose, take over the property and sell.

Let's step it back a little. The original owner of the mortgage note has now made a total profit of $79,960 plus the newly collected $150,000. That's a total of $229,960 from simply giving out a loan of $500,000 in cash.

Unfortunately, that was a 3.83% annual return on investment of that money. But it's better than a loss. At least, the original $500,000 was recouped back with some profit to do more business.

Besides, this is probably one of many mortgage loans issued out with the majority performing well and returning much more. Imagine a fully matured and paid off loan through a full term of 30 years. The total paid back on the loan would be $966,279. It's one of the safest forms of investment that returns more than 6% on an annual basis.

Oftentimes, these mortgage types of investments are also protected by insurance and certain laws; again, such as the ability to foreclose on the collateral. It's an awesome way to park money and create safe returns.

What happens to the new investor who purchased the $300,000 promissory note at $150,000? First of all, the collateral is $450,000. Imagine if the investor decides after 12 months of unsuccessful collection activities to foreclose on the property.

It's very unlikely that a full $450,000 will be realized from a foreclosure auction sale. Let's assume a worst case scenario whereby the property sold at $300,000. In that instance, the investor would have just doubled an initial investment of $150,000 in just one year.

Why won't the original lender do this? The simple answer is "time value." Sometimes, it's better to save time than to save money. In fact, it's often much more profitable to do so. Time is more valuable than money.

This is especially true because the bank specializes in flipping money and not long term investment in mortgages. They are also not in the business of property management.

So the last thing that the bank wants is to foreclose and take over a property. They would rather sell the mortgage at market value and move on to newer projects which are usually initiating and originating new mortgage loans.

Big institutions do this all day long packaging multiple mortgage loans together and selling them in bulk. In fact, there are derivatives of this trade being traded as securities on Wall Street. When you understand how this works, you gain a whole new respect for the power of real estate.

Investors that purchase mortgage notes also have the option of contacting the mortgagor and arranging loan modifications and workout plans that can turn them to performing assets. As you can imagine, people default on mortgages sometimes because of life circumstances beyond their control.

As an investor who just purchased a non-performing note at half its original value, you may have found a borrower who wants an arrangement to start paying again. You can refinance into a deal that drops their monthly payment from $2,685 to $2,500. You can structure the deal in a way that can benefit you and the borrower and still create meaningful profits.

Anytime you create solutions that move money around, you create value and therefore profits are made. On the contrary, stagnant money produces nothing. In fact, it loses value because of the value of time and inevitable inflation.

Mortgage notes are powerful investments primarily because they are backed, insured and protected by an underlying collateral. What that means is that the balance attached to the promissory note will always be due during the transfer of deed and ownership. There are so many ways you can get creative with promissory notes.

Here is an example. Back in 2006, my partner and I sold a property where we basically had to walk away with almost nothing. It was the most profitable thing to do.

When we got to the closing, we discovered some liens that had not come to our awareness. They had to be paid. In order for the deal to go through, we had to let go of our profit of about $23,000 and walk away with nothing.

However, the end buyer was willing to give us a mortgage note for $23,000. It was recorded at the county house just like the other documents such as the first mortgage and the deed.

I thought to myself; *"I would never see that money again."* But it was more profitable and better to let go. Holding on to the property would cost us money in holding cost and the responsibility of having to maintain the property. That wasn't the business I was in. I was a real estate wholesaler and a "fix and flip" investor.

Less than 2 years later, I received a call from my partner. He told me to expect a check of $5,000 in the mail as the property had been sold. Due to the recorded mortgage note of $23,000, we were offered a short pay off of $10,000. It was of course smart to accept that money and move on. This is just one of the powers of mortgage notes in its more mini form.

In the next chapter, we will start getting into the various entry strategies, their pros and cons. We've talked about the goals and how to plan profit ahead of the deals. It's time to discover how to find the deals.

Let's go there.

SECTION 3

ENTRY STRATEGIES

(FINDING THE DEALS)

CHAPTER 12

On & Off-Market Deals

When it comes to finding deals, you have to think on your feet and often out of the box. However there are a few tips I can give as context to help you with that. On a grand scheme, deals can be found on or off the market.

When a property is on the market, that means its owner is actively seeking a buyer or seeking to sell the property. The seller is actively marketing the deal to more people and there is exposure for the deal. Naturally, it will attract more eyeballs if it's in fact a good deal.

There are certain cases where a bidding war may even happen. That means multiple people bidding to purchase the property. Increase in demand will obviously create an increase in perceived value.

From a basic economic standpoint, the intrinsic value of the property can get lost in a shuffle when faced with a bidding war situation. But you should expect to be faced with that challenge when a property has already been made available before your interest in purchasing it.

If everything else were equal, on-market deals means overpaying for the property. But as always, there are exceptions to the rule. These exceptions are available when opportunities to add value to certain types of properties is not a popular or mainstream practice.

On the market, you can find ugly houses that need rehab and repair. Those properties are listed on the market but the majority of potential buyers don't go to the market to look for such houses. Majority go to the market to fall in love emotionally with a home; not a house and not a property.

So as for you in research to find real estate money secrets, you already know to focus on looking for opportunities to add value. When you go into a marketplace looking for a home to fall in love emotionally with, you are essentially looking to get value.

That is walking backwards away from creating income. That's the behavior of consumers. You should always be focused on being more of the producer.

So in this case, the exception when looking at on-market deals is to look for opportunities to add value. Look for ugly unwanted deals that the mainstream does not want. Your opportunity lies in the desire to turn the property into what the consumers want.

These types of properties are often listed as fixer uppers, needs TLC (which stands for tender loving care), need repairs etc. Sometimes the listing will say that buyers are responsible for the %.

What is %?

% is the certificate of occupancy which is a document issued by the city's building department certifying a building's compliance with applicable building codes and other laws, and indicating it to be in a condition suitable for occupancy.

Typically, pretty homes listed on the market will guarantee occupancy compliance. So that's a value that consumers want. When a property is listed without already having this stuff, nobody wants it.

That also means low mainstream demand whereby you can negotiate offers low enough to add value and make money. These are the only properties on the market that you can make quick profits from.

There is nothing wrong with purchasing a home at retail value on the market. If it's the home you are going to live in, you absolutely should want it if you are willing and able to pay for it. It's not just a house; it's the home where you lay your head.

As for the home you are going to live in, the money in it is made in the long term in the form of equity. A percentage of your monthly mortgage payment goes towards building the equity over time. In addition to that, real estate has historically grown in value.

The best deals are off-market deals. It only makes sense that the best of the best deals have to be uncovered and not already public. If there is exposure for it already, there is obviously higher demand if it's such a good deal.

Again, it's another similar value opportunity situation. Everytime you want ready-made value, you will pay more. If you are willing to add or create value, you will pay less and you can sell the value for more.

When you learn how to find off-market deals, you will be the only one at the negotiation table all the time. If you let others get the deal into the market, you have to pay their fees directly or indirectly. So how do you find off-market deals?

The first thing I need to make clear is that it's not about convincing people to sell a home that they don't already want to sell. In fact, convincing will put you in a very weak position of negotiation.

Instead, we will focus on people who want to sell or are thinking of selling but haven't yet decided. These people are already on a fence and all you are doing is helping them get off the fence. People can be on the fence especially during certain types of *"not so fortunate"* events.

Here are some of those events:

Preforeclosures - Sometimes, homeowners find themselves in situations in which they can't financially meet obligations that may include mortgage payments. There are generous grace periods that simply may not be enough to catch up with. They can't make the payment.

It can happen in the short term, it may take a long time and some will never catch up. If an owner is not able to catch up in 3 months, the mortgage bank files a document at the court called lis pendens. It's basically an official intention to foreclose.

At this stage, it becomes a public record. Basically anyone with interest has access to list of preforeclosures. You can also market your offer to this list until you create a seller.

The banks don't actually foreclose until up to 12 months after last payment is received. The owner remains the legal owner of the deed until actual foreclosure. During that period, any one can send letters to these properties in efforts to purchase the property.

This is called direct mailing. In order for this to work on an average, direct mailing has to be done in volume. Basically, I wouldn't send less than 100 letters at any given deployment.

Divorce - There are more than 50% divorce in this age of increasing civilization. Couples usually end up having to liquidate properties they acquired and owned together. That usually means a home and sometimes 2nd, 3rd and 4th home.

Most people are able to afford their home only because they have a second income source from a spouse. When there is a split, one of the first obligations that become unbearable is the mortgage payment. That means a need to downsize.

When you have to offload properties this way, time is often not a luxury. One or both of them usually wants to escape the pain and misery that come with such marriage and the divorce as fast as they can. That presents an opportunity to make an offer low enough to make profit in flipping the property or creating inbuilt equity.

Just like preforeclosures, lists of divorce and divorce-d cases are usually public records. Just like many law firms, you can market to these individuals and walk away with good properties at $0.50 - $0.60 (cents) on the dollar; or even lower. It's simple but it takes dedication.

Probate - This is a source of deal corresponding to property inheritances that heirs want to dispose of. The public announcement of finalizing a will is what is referred to as probate. Inside this public document, you can find information about these new owners and you can market to them using direct mailing.

You can also reach out to these potential leads by researching their phone numbers and calling them directly. Either way, it's a numbers game. We will talk about how I reach out in a later chapter.

Often, when people inherit these properties, they don't want to live in them. Some would rather just sell the property and walk away. If they do decide to sell, they usually want just enough unlike a home that a seller is emotionally attached to.

When you market to these types of off-market deals, you are usually the only one at the negotiation table. It's a very powerful position to be in. Make your offer, justify it and get the contract signed.

When you are the only potential buyer, all you have to worry about is building rapport. You don't have to worry about competition and bidding wars.

If you can manage to get the seller to like you, they will trust your judgment and walk away with your offer. After all, they didn't really work personally to acquire the property.

As usual, you need numbers on your side to enjoy this process of finding deals. If you are doing this one property after the other, your spirit will get burnt out as most people will not be interested in your offer. It's a numbers and volume game.

Tax Delinquency, Bankruptcy and Expired Listings are three additional sources of off-market deals that you can capitalize on. Same methods of contacting them apply. You can send letters, you can knock on these doors and you can call if you find their phone numbers.

You can find homeowner phone numbers using a process called skip tracing but it's still a numbers game. You also have to know how to build rapport over the phone and set appointments to see the property.

For me personally, I prefer marketing enough to generate inbound calls. Again, we will discuss further on the best reach out methods in a later chapter dedicated to that.

There are also ways for you to find homeowners with high equity. That means they owe much less than the property is worth. These can create great opportunities to buy cheaply from folks who do not have time to wait for retail buyers.

My least favorite people to reach out to are *"for sale by owners"*. These are folks who have decided to list on a website in hopes to save the cost of using an agent. They usually are not as motivated as I need them to be to sell.

In the next chapter, we will talk a little bit about auctions, sheriff and foreclosure sales. There are a few pros and cons that you should be aware of.

In general, I avoid them and I will share why with you.

Let's keep it moving.

CHAPTER 13

Auctions, Sheriff & Foreclosure Sales

One of the questions I get the most is "how do I buy foreclosures?" When people ask me that question, it's usually because they've heard from some guru or online that real estate in foreclosure is cheaper.

While that can be true, it can also turn out to be a total disaster. Do I really want to share the horror stories with you now? Not really. But in this chapter, I felt I needed to share some tips in simple layman language to help you avoid common mistakes.

I covered everything before this part to encourage you of many other options to enter into real estate investment. Under no circumstances should you ever feel the need to invest in a property you have not inspected unless it's an investment in a trust or partnership funds. I wanted to make that clear. With that out of the way, let's break down the foreclosure thing.

The foreclosure process starts at the very moment a monthly mortgage payment defaults. But the foreclosure doesn't actually happen until 10-12 months later. Foreclosure process period varies from state to state in the United States.

Between the point that a payment defaults and the actual foreclosure sale represents a big window of opportunity to buy an investment that you get to inspect. If you wait till after it's been foreclosed on, you will have to buy at the sheriff auction sale. At this stage, you may not be allowed to inspect the property.

If you are well experienced, you may choose to take certain types of risk. Personally, there are so many options to invest in. So I think there is absolutely never a reason for me to invest my money or investors' money into a property we can't inspect first.

The idea in this chapter is to clarify the differences between auctions, Sheriff sales and foreclosure. Foreclosure is a process. Auction and Sheriff sales are one time events.

The very last event in the foreclosure process where you can acquire a property is the Sheriff sale and/or auction. Depending on the jurisdiction or state, Sheriff sale and auction may be the same or slightly different. Whatever the differences are is mainly legal stuff and you can always learn by asking.

There are a few stages *(pretty similar in most developed and civilized society)* to note:

1. Lis Pendens
2. Preforeclosure
3. Foreclosure Sale
4. REO or Bank Owned

Lis Pendens - This stage happens usually three months after defaulting on a mortgage payment. When a property owner hasn't paid the mortgage payment in 3 consecutive months, the notice filed at the courthouse is called lis pendens.

It means a pending lawsuit. Some states call it intention to foreclose. The terminology varies a bit but it's the same idea. Either way, the mortgage payment default becomes public record.

Pre-Foreclosure - Once lis pendens (*or whatever the first document related to the default*) is filed at the courthouse, the pre foreclosure period has started. During this period, the owner remains the legal holder of the deed and continues to have the right to the property.

This is a moment when they can decide to sell the property with a real motivation to sell cheaply. In addition to being able to pick up great deals, you can still inspect the property to ensure that you don't lock yourself in a bad situation.

Let's put some perspective on that. What's a bad situation? One of my clients purchased a property from an online auction. Yes, those exist now too.

There are online real estate auction websites such as realtybid, hubzu etc. There are instructions with these auction listings that typically warn against trespassing. In addition to that, all sales are final or you can lose your deposits if you change your mind.

Anyway, my client bought a property from one of these sites. He ended up with a property that had an old oil tank underground that had a big leak. Due to environmental laws and regulations, the soil had to be tested and cleaned in order to get a proper certification.

After much deliberation back and forth, he ended up with a bill of $400,000. This is a devastating and horrible position to ever find one's self. Unless you have experience in the neighborhood as an investor, I would not be buying a property that can't be walked through for inspection at least once before closing a deal. For the record, he became my client after that horrible experience.

Foreclosure Sale - At this stage, the mortgage bank has exhausted the collection activities designed to try to bring the mortgage back-current. So the courts have given the go ahead to sell the property at a sales auction.

In New Jersey's most counties, there is a weekly auction event. It's the same day every week and the list of properties to auction has already been published for the public.

At the auction, the listed price is the principal balance of the loan that defaulted. In a lot of cases, the bank can't find a buyer willing to pay up to the principal balance. Here is an example.

John's property is being auctioned. He owes $150,000 so the sheriff listed the property to be auctioned for $150,000 plus related fees. Even though the property value had been estimated at $120,000, the highest bid at the auction was $63,000.

This is yet another reason why the bank doesn't enjoy foreclosing. So the bank decided to buy the house at the Sheriff foreclosure auction sale. That's when the property becomes an REO.

REO or Bank Owned - The bank foreclosed but with having to buy back the property itself. After that, the bank orders a BPO (broker's price opinion) to determine an official professional opinion of the property value.

Then the property is listed on the MLS at or a little below its value for the public market to make offers on. We will discuss this in detail in the next chapter. We will be talking about relationships with agencies and brokers and how to leverage them to find deals.

Overall, the foreclosure process presents a great opportunity to find awesome deals. But the main gist is to avoid buying properties without some kind of upfront inspection. Sure you can get lucky but luck and hope are terrible business strategies.

CHAPTER 14

Agency & M.L.S

Earlier in the book, I clarified the differences between on and off-market deals. Buying and selling real estate can become very complicated without the right people and entities on your real estate team. Having an agency and access to the MLS is a great leverage point for both buyers and sellers.

The real estate market is truly vast and dynamic, with daily fluctuations. Some people's livelihoods depend on these market fluctuations. Due to this fact, it's highly beneficial for you to stay educated in real-time on market values. The closest thing to the most professional opinion of market values is provided by licensed agencies through the multiple listing systems (THE MLS).

Traditionally, the MLS was a system accessible only to licensed real estate brokers and agents. However, with the emergence of websites such as Zillow, Trulia, Redfin, and others, that's becoming more of a thing of the past. Access to more information is now available to anyone with enough interest.

Data is everywhere, and more of it is collected as we live our daily lives in real-time. A common example of this is the data collection that occurs every time you use GPS while driving. By agreeing to and using the device, you are collecting data that other users can use to make intelligent decisions about directions while driving.

With such access, you can also find contact information, the number of days a property has been on the market, and other information that provides intelligence related to the value of a property. For example, when a property sits on the market for sale for more than 100 days, it's an indication that it's worth less than what the seller thought.

The market is always right. If the market indicates a lack of interest in a property by not generating offers, it's not just a truth; it's the reality of the property's value. The best source for this level of information is an agency and, effectively, the MLS.

As a buyer, the MLS is a source of intelligent market information. As a seller, it creates extensive market exposure for your property. Basically, there is a cost associated with avoiding the services of an agency and not leveraging the MLS.

Let's take a $100,000 property, for example. Agents typically charge 2.5% - 3% to list properties for sale. So, if you decide to sell it, the first step is to call a licensed real estate agent. The listing agreement stipulates that when the property sells, 2.5% of the sales price will be deducted from the sales proceeds as fees or sales commission for the agent.

2.5% of $100,000 = $2,500

A good agent will create a compelling presentation of your property for viewing and inspection, both visually and informatively. Then, the property will be listed on the MLS for maximum exposure. This also means that other agents licensed to work in the area can bring buyers to your property. In simple terms, you have every agent working for you, and all you have to pay is the 2.5%. Isn't that an awesome deal?

Also, note that the higher the sales price, the more your sales proceeds will be, and more importantly, the more sales commissions the agent will earn. This means that the agent has a vested interest in getting you more money.

If the agent can get you $150,000, that's $50,000 more in sales proceeds. The agent will work diligently to get you that extra $50,000 simply because they want that extra $1,250.

What's the alternative? I know that technology is improving every day, and it may seem like any individual can list their own house on the internet. It's called *"for sale by owner,"* and yes, it's possible for a property to *"sell by owner"*.

But can it be sold earlier and for more money with an agent via the MLS? Definitely yes! This is especially true because agents work hard to achieve this for you.

With *"for sale by owner"* listings, some agencies allow clients to pay a flat fee for exposure to the MLS market. As usual, nothing is impossible with technology. However, the seller will have to take on responsibilities such as sales presentation, staging, and negotiating offers.

So the services of an agency and exposure to the MLS, whether as a buyer or seller, cannot hurt you. But the lack thereof can definitely hurt you without your knowledge. So it makes sense to leverage both whenever you can.

One of the best things about agencies is that there is no charge unless your desired result is achieved. If it costs you nothing to use them, just use them. It simply means a bigger team for all your real estate endeavors.

You can even take it a step further. Get licensed as a real estate agent. It's another aspect of this industry that can only help you. You can be a part-timer who simply makes money from referrals to full-timers. The only regulatory requirement is full disclosure when personally engaged in a transaction as a buyer or seller.

In the next chapter, I will share the best way for you to find awesome deals. Not many people are talking about this strategy, but I believe that's precisely why I should share it with you. It's a method that will position you to leverage the #1 secret of the game: consistency.

CHAPTER 15

Online Ads & P.P.C

Most people who struggle to make headway with investing in real estate do so because they don't know how to consistently fill the pipeline with new seller prospects. Some of those who have some experience get stuck using old-school methods of finding deals.

Being old-school doesn't mean it doesn't work; it means its efficiency and effectiveness in an ever-evolving, technology-driven age are questionable. Online ad platforms and pay-per-click advertising are the saving grace. Let's go through a few examples.

I remember when I launched my real estate investment business back in 2005. I was fortunate enough to have learned from some mentors who emphasized the importance of marketing as a consistent source of deals. But what is marketing, and what does it have to do with real estate?

Real estate wealth is created when you cash out on equity built over time or when you buy a property at a price lower than its current market value. As shown previously in this book, there are also creative ways to create cashable value in real estate. But all of them rely on your ability to attract people to whom you can add some type of value.

Let's be clear. It's not about attracting real estate; it's about your ability to attract people. When we send out letters, hang signs, knock on doors, cold call; all of it is an attempt to attract people from whom we will buy or to whom we will sell property, and hopefully, that translates to value for them. Said value can be cash sales proceeds or simply peace of mind.

These are old-school ways of attracting people, also known as motivated sellers. There are much more effective ways to scale marketing efforts to attract people these days. My favorite is through online ads via platforms such as Google and Facebook Ads.

This strategy is called Pay-Per-Click advertising or PPC for short. If you are like most people, you have one or two social media profiles that you spend a significant amount of time on per day. But let's look at the statistics.

> "1.47 billion people on average log onto Facebook daily and are considered daily active users (Facebook DAU) for June 2018, which represents an 11 percent increase year over year" (Source: Facebook as 07/25/18).

60% of Facebook's audience would be considered DAU versus Monthly Active Users (MAU). The fact of the matter is that the audience you need to be marketing to is actively on social media on a daily basis.

Facebook, Google, and many other online platforms allow you to advertise at scale to these audiences at a rate much cheaper than traditional methods. It's important to also note why it's cheaper. With the technology available today, every response to advertising can be tracked down to the interest level.

That means you can track and tweak your ongoing campaigns according to response rates. If it's working out, you scale up, and if not, you can stop it. The response and interest level can be tracked at any level starting from the very first click into ads. That's why it's called pay-per-click.

You only pay when there is an interest, evident by a click into the ad on the websites and social media. If there is no interest, you don't have to pay a penny. But you will collect meaningful data to use in creating a marketing message compelling enough to attract people.

For example, you will know exactly how many people saw your ad. You will also know how many actually clicked on it. The percentage of the number of people who clicked to the number of people who saw it is called the click-through rate (CTR). The higher the CTR is, the more responsive your marketing message is.

The best part about that is that the advertising media platform is also rooting for you. When your CTR is high, they use that data as an indication that their users are happy to see your message. Their algorithms reward you with a lower cost per click (CPC) for that.

With the old-school methods, you have to work and spend money before you can find out if it works or not. As you can imagine, a lot of resources, including cash, energy, and time, can be managed and preserved better with online and PPC advertising. Your efforts can yield a lot more.

Considering these new opportunities, direct mailing through the post office is overpriced. With traditional street bandit signs, many cities consider it littering. In fact, I personally have received multiple calls from city code enforcement threatening me with a $1,500 fine for hanging these signs. That's not my idea of freedom.

Last but not least, the number one secret to making money in real estate is consistency. One of the hardest things for human beings is consistency. Therefore, it's very important to position yourself for consistency when advertising your message of *"I buy houses."*

Responses to most of the old-school advertising methods are luck and hope-based. *"Hope deferred makes the heart weak."* While there are testimonials of people who have successfully used them, myself included, most people just wait and wait until they quit.

For example, cold calling positions you to, borderline, have to beg. That is what I mean by positioning for consistency. Consistency is simply easier in certain positions.

However, I strongly suggest that you close your first to fourth deals using cold calling to distressed homeowners. Yes, it's hard, but it will build your confidence with respect to talking to prospects and negotiation skills. We cover this in our mastermind www.myempirepro/com/blog/masterclass step by step in detail to make it easier.

After closing your first deal, you can scale up by hiring virtual assistants to call all your data/leads first, to screen for a desire to sell or not. Then, they can schedule appointments for call-backs from you.

Once you are consistently closing 2-3 deals monthly, you can then scale your marketing to online ads and PPC. You can even afford to add direct mailing at this point in your real estate investing career.

When you set up ads that are compelling enough to attract the right sellers, they reach out to you. Being in the position where people get to reach out to you for your offer is better and more powerful. You and anyone can do that all day long.

Find your favorite exit and entry strategy and do them consistently. My personal favorite is setting up ads online that simply offer *"offers for homes in any condition"* in my targeted geographical location as identified by zip and postal codes. PPC and online advertising make real estate investing a lot more fun after paying your dues, of course.

CHAPTER 16

7 KEYS TO SUCCESS

As you have discovered thus far, real estate presents a lot of income opportunities for both short and long term. Everyone is familiar with the idea of being a landlord, building a rental portfolio and collecting passive income. Is it truly passive?

Let me remind you that there is a difference between being a landlord and being a real estate investor. One is a day job (hint: landlordship) where you can potentially lose money trying to be an apartment superintendent combined with investing. The other allows you to build wealth; Being an investor where your money works for you.

Either way, these 7 key concepts that I am about to share with you are paramount. They are designed to protect you from losing money in real estate investing. It is more of a miracle to <u>not</u> lose money attempting real estate investing than it is it to lose money.

Real estate is a lucrative sector of any society's economy and ecosystem. Building wealth with it is extremely simple but so is losing money because people naturally approach it with so much speculation and the complicated nature of human beings.

YES. Real estate has historically appreciated in value over history. However there have been ups and downs that can bury dreams alive. You do not need speculation because there is more than enough data available to make intelligent decisions.

So while becoming a rental investor is awesome for the long term, you must also engage in strategies that will help you increase your net worth in leaps and faster. If you are an average person, you are starting your real estate investing journey with less than $100,000 in capital. I know it probably took you a while to save that money but it is not a lot of money.

However it is more than enough to build a million dollar empire in less than 5 years. If all you are doing is buying rental properties at market value, it may take forever. So in addition to building a rental portfolio, I recommend that you add *"fix and flip"* as an investing strategy to your tool box. We covered the strategy in chapter 8.

It's essentially the art and science of buying properties that need repair, hiring contractors to repair the property and then selling it for a profit. Please note that I did not say anything about doing the repair D.I.Y as you see on HGTV.

For example, you bought a property at $60,000. You spent $10,000 on repairs making it a total of $70,000 in total investment. You then sold it at $100,000. You made a gross profit of $30,000.

If you do 2 projects in one year like this, you would have turn $140,000 to $200,000. That's an annual return on investment of approximately 43%. At that rate, how long will it take you to double your initial investment?

Let's use the rule of 72.

*"The **Rule of 72** is a simple way to determine how long an investment will take to double given a fixed annual rate of interest. By dividing **72** by the annual rate of return, investors obtain a rough estimate of how many years it will take for the initial investment to duplicate itself."*

Therefore 72 divided by 43 = 1.67 years.

That's about 20 months. So ideally, every 20 months ideally, you can double your money. This is only possible for an average man in real estate *"fix and flip"* investment.

If you had spent that same $140,000 on buying a rental property at an annual cap rate of 9%, you would generate $11,200 in net operating income annually. How long will it take you to double that money?

It will take you (72 divided by 9) 8 Years to double that money with buying rental property alone as opposed to less than 2 years in *"buy, fix and flip"* deals. That's more than 4 times longer to flip your money for the same results.

What's the catch with the latter? It requires a robust machine with the 7 keys that I want to share with you to mitigate the risk associated with it as a short term real estate investing strategy. *"Buy, fix and rent"* is more of a long term investing strategy that seems very safe.

As a solution expert in real estate investing, a lot of my clients became clients because they got in trouble with buying rental properties. Therefore rental investments are not as safe as some make it out to be.

It still requires diligence with just a quarter of the results you get in *"fix and flips"* to show for it. The verdict is to build a portfolio of both strategies over the long term. Engage in at least 2 *"buy, fix and flips"* per year and retain the best of them to rent out for long term passive income.

That's diversification at its best.

The banks are only open to lending you and I money to invest in real estate. The banks do not loan money for investing in stocks, crypto, currency, your 401K, CDs etc. They only lend money for investing in real estate.

That presents an extension to this massive opportunity. For every dollar you have available to invest in real estate, the bank is open to giving you additional $3 or more to make money from. It's the most secured form of collateral. In fact, it's an investment for them.

That benefit alone dramatically changes how fast you can increase your net worth because your purchasing power is quadrupled. Your money can then go even further. Here is a simple example.

Instead of investing that $140,000 in just 2 projects as illustrated in the first example, you can now invest $560,000 [$140,000 + ($140,000 x 3)]. That covers the cost of 8 different projects in a year.

The bank is doing this primarily because they want to share your profits with you; of course. The bank wants 15 cents ($0.15) back for every dollar they lend to your projects. You will keep the rest of any profits made. Let's do some quick math.

For simplicity, the projects will get the same 43% return on investment. So with an investment of $560,000, the gross profit will be approximately $240,800.

The bank gives you $420,000 for these 8 projects but they expect 15% of that money back in interest. That's $63,000. So let's deduct that from the gross profit of $240,800. [$240,800 - $63,000] = $177,800.

You invested the same cash initial investment of $140,000 in order to make $60,000 earlier but that same amount has now made you $177,800. Basically, you increase your results by almost 200% by simply leveraging the banks' money. I know. It's awesome.

What is the actual cash-on-cash return on your initial investment? ($177,800/$140,000) x 100% = 127%. At that R.O.I rate, how long will it take to double your initial investment? 72/127 = 0.6 year; which is basically a little over half of one year (6-7 months).

Therefore, a combination of real estate and leverage is key to building your purchasing power and liquidity very fast. As long as you know the 7 keys that I want to share with you and its application, you are safe.

Keep in mind that with *"buy, fix and flips"*, there are transactional fees such as lender points, closing costs, realty transfer fees, taxes, holding expenses, interests payments, agent commissions, etc that accounts for another 10%-15%.

Therefore your original 43% profit is probably more like 27%-33% R.O.I. But even at that, it will take you under 3 years to double your initial investment if you are paying all cash and faster if you are leveraging the bank's money as you should.

Let's talk about the 7 Keys.

1. Knowledge

Congratulations. Reading this book is a great first step towards continuing education and increasing the ever-evolving knowledge required to succeed in real estate investing. There are new discoveries from year to year and generation to generation. You have to stay on top of it.

2. Experience

The best form of education is in 'doing' and experience. There are a few ways to acquire experience. You can make tons of mistakes and waste thousands of dollars like we did in the beginning.

But you can also, avoid wasting money, engage and leverage apprenticeship from a mentor and partnerships with people who have experience in exchange for splitting profits; all day long.

3. Skills

As you practice more and more, you build more skills in the game which you will need in order to outpace everyone else indefinitely. With skills, you are able to optimize the consumption of time and/or energy competitively when getting tasks done.

I can't tell you how many newbies who lose money daily because of lack of skills; thousands of dollars of their own money. It's mind-boggling. Beyond that, they are losing the bank's money 3 to 5 times even more; which means digging a financial grave for themselves even before they get started or make money.

Skills can only be acquired over 'time' and never instantly. The only way that can be close to "instant" is by forming a team with others who have acquired it over time. You save 'time' achieving meaningful results by acquired skills from 'time' and experience in the business.

4. System

With experience and skills, one can only come across so many issues. After a while, the issues that come up are the same or of the same type. The problem is that just one or a few issues can take your business out; dead.

Building a knowledge base of potential issues and mode of operation around the knowledge is what I am referring to as a system here. *"A system is a group of interactive and interrelated entities that form a unified whole."*

In order to form a unified whole that multiplies money by way of real estate investing, you need to have a system. The system needs to be enriched with intelligence of all the potential issues.

Such issues include and are not limited to closing problems, title records, hiring, dealing with and firing contractors, pricing and valuing properties properly, satisfying loan and insurance underwriters, dealing with building codes and much more.

If I could show you my real estate, entrepreneurship and business "body", you would see bullet wounds and scars of all types all over it. I am one of the lucky few who refused to allow that to assassinate my career and ambitions of building an empire with real estate. Instead, I've built a whole system out of it and part of it is what you are learning in this book so that you can leverage it.

5. Time to Manage

Being a landlord requires more time than a full time job. Likewise, being a project manager for *'fix and flips'* requires more time than a full time job. The gurus may have painted it as a lifestyle business with freedom of time. That couldn't be further from the truth.

When you watch 'fix and flip' tv shows on HGTV, they compress quite a bit of how much time is required into a 20 or 40 minute show. If you want to be a successful real estate investor, focus on being an investor and not a landlord, superintendent, project manager or general contractor.

Simply learn the simple math of initial investment capital, projected revenue and the rate of return on investment. All it takes is to leverage your money and credit worthiness in partnership with those who have systems in place. With that formula, very little time is required and you can then focus on bringing in more income, multiplying it while avoiding as much cost of learning curve as possible.

If you have the luxury of time, there is a very high chance that you do not have the luxury of a decent investment capital or credit worthiness. It doesn't matter. A good mentor will help you identify where you are lacking and show you how to use partnership and joint venture to supplement it. That's the beauty of real estate.

6. Credit and credibility

Speaking of the beauty of real estate, it's the only investment vehicle that the bank will lend you money as leverage to invest in. However, in order to be able to do so at a decent interest rate, you need a good credit score.

"A credit score is a numerical expression based on a level analysis of a person's credit files, to represent the creditworthiness of an individual."

Credit scores range from 250 - 900. Any score above 650 will typically attract a decent interest rate. The higher the interest rate, the higher the cost of building wealth with leverage in real estate will be. As shown previously, the ability to leverage the banks' money will potentially increase your returns on investment by almost 200%.

If you have bad credit, it's easier now more than ever before to clean up your credit records and build a clean profile. You can even do so at a very small fraction of what you may owe. You may even find that you do not have to pay a dime back. There are great and cheap resources for doing so today.

7. Cash and Capital

Here is a quick warning. If you clean your credit without building income and financial independence, you will only mess up the credit again. If I had to choose between building my income and fixing my credit, I will always choose building my income as it automatically leads to having a good and excellent credit in addition to having cash as seed capital.

Even though you have the opportunity to leverage the bank's money, they require, for the most part, that you have some skin in the game. If they don't, it becomes too costly and can lead to what we call over-leverage which is primarily the cause of personal and economy-wide recessions.

If you don't have any capital, real estate presents opportunities to engage in partnership-based investing hack strategies such as wholesaling and bird-dogging to create income and raise lucrative cash. But these strategies required time and marketing skills; more time than most people on a full time job are able and/or willing to give the business.

But with some capital, you can keep your day job as the income generator for today's needs but also as seeds to multiply using partnerships. That leads me to some bonus keys you can leverage to build wealth in real estate.

Bonus - Partnership, Action and Consistency.

If you have been paying attention, you would have noticed a consistent theme thus far; **"partnership"**. If you are missing any part of the 7 keys right now, simply create a strategic partnership with others in real estate who have them.

So in reality, you have access to all 7 keys already and we've also made it easy to network and partner with others in the real estate investing business. In fact, the first major lesson I learn in real estate is to join a local meetup and that's where I met my first mentor.

It made it easier for me to commit to taking action and remaining consistent. Consistency is not easy. It's one of the hardest things for humans to achieve. Being able to take action and do it consistently will increase your odds of ending up in the top 1% wealthiest of human beings.

With the 7 keys and this bonus, you will become unstoppable. You will have all the resources you need to pull off successful real estate investments. You can flip to fast cash as well as hold for long term passive income.

To partner with us with your time to create income, simply visit www.myempirepro.com/masterclass and come inside through the masterclass.

CONCLUSION

Writing this book has been an awesome experience for me. You know what they say about teaching. When you teach, you learn twice.

My goal was to hopefully shed some light on a few of the many opportunities that real estate presents. Historically, it remains the realest form of asset that can house your net worth and value.

It will be a very sad thing to end your real estate journey in this book. Your knowledge has hopefully increased just a tad bit. But it's time to implement and execute on this material; take consistent action.

I get questions all the time. The question that I get the most is however this. *"Ola, how do I get started in the real estate game?"* The answer varies from person to person and from individual to individual.

Because of that, I've decided to make myself available to you via my website www.myempirepro.com/masterclass

All you have to do is attend the free masterclass and you can get started wherever you are.

The only requirement that I enforce is to read this book first. That's why I made it so affordable. I want anyone and everyone to be able to access this information and be able to change their lives.

In your position and particular financial profile, your first step may be to buy a home to live in. Just keep in mind that I am against paying full price for a house. Maybe it's to expand your rental portfolio or maybe it's to create short term but lucrative income from buying to flip. On the free consulting, we will both figure that out.

So go ahead and book your session with me and we will take it from there. Knowledge is not power until you implement it. Let's get you going.

www.myempirepro.com/masterclass

REFERENCES

Big Data for Real Estate Tailored For You
www.EmpireBigData.com

FREE Wholesale Real Estate Course
www.myEmpirePRO.com/freerealestatecourse

List Building Autoresponder
www.myEmpirePRO.com/autoresponder

Digital Marketing Certified
www.DigitalMarketingCertified.com

Real Estate Money Secrets by OLA
www.RealEstateMoneySecrets.com

Get My Marriage Back by LOLA & OLA
www.GetMyMarriageBack.com

Watch This Book as Videos on YouTube.
www.myempirepro.com/srew-on-youtube

WordPress Hosting
www.myEmpirePRO.com/hosting

NOTES FROM MASTERCLASS

Masterclass Here: www.myEmpirePRO.com/masterclass

NOTES

NOTES

NOTES

NOTES

NOTES

NOTES

www.ingramcontent.com/pod-product-compliance
Lightning Source LLC
Chambersburg PA
CBHW021814170526
45157CB00007B/2589